ROYAL LONDON IN CONTEXT

The Independent Traveler's Guide to Royal London

ROYAL LONDON
IN CONTEXT

The Independent Traveler's Guide to Royal London

By

Robert S. Wayne

**INDEPENDENT
INTERNATIONAL
TRAVEL, LLC**

The second offering in the *Europe In Context* series

www.europeincontext.com

(left) Member of the Household Cavalry Regiment, Blues and Royals.

Author: Robert S. Wayne
Published by Independent International Travel, LLC© 2004

Disclaimer:
The author and publisher have made their best efforts to confirm the most current data prior to publication. Prices, opening and closing times, and services are subject to change at any time. Readers should confirm prices, facilities, availabilities, services, and times when they arrive at their destination. If you find anything has changed, or you want to share your travel experiences or photographs of your trip, please contact us by E-mail at **europeincontext@mindspring.com**

Visit our Web site, **www.europeincontext.com**
Or you can send mail to
Independent International Travel, LLC
201 Swanton Way
Decatur, Georgia 30030

ISBN 0-9720228-8-0
Publisher's Cataloging-in Publication Data
(Provided by Quality Books)

Wayne, Robert S.
  Royal London in context : the independent traveler's guide to royal London/by Robert S. Wayne.
  p. cm. --(Europe in context; 2)
  Includes bibliographical references and index.
  ISBN 0-9720228-8-0

  1. London (England)--Guidebooks. 2. London (England) --History. 3. Great Britain--Kings and rulers.
  I. Title.
  DA679.W39 2004   914.2104'86
                          QBI03-200718

Library of Congress Catalogue Card Number: 2003112684

Distributed to the trade exclusively by
Independent Publishers Group
814 North Franklin St.
Chicago, IL 60610
Phone: (312) 337-0747/Orders Only (800) 888-4741
Orders: orders@ipgbook.com/Customer Service: frontdesk@ipgbook.com

Front Cover: Queen Elizabeth II is escorted to Buckingham Palace during the 2003 Trooping the Color Parade. Reuters NewsMedia Inc./CORBIS
Proofreading and editing by Rebecca Landers and Bright Direction
CD Recording made at Allgood Studios, Atlanta, Georgia
Cover design, maps, and diagrams by Renny Hart
Printed and bound in Italy by L.E.G.O.

FOREWORD

Royal London In Context follows *Venice In Context* as the second book in the *Europe In Context* series. Just as travelers are drawn to the glorious art and architecture of Venice, visitors to London are often intrigued by British royalty. Many are fascinated by its traditions and delight in the pomp and pageantry of its ancient ceremonies. Perhaps we remember a smattering of English history from school, but our impressions of its kings and queens have been shaped by countless Hollywood films such as *The Lion In Winter* starring Peter O'Toole and Katherine Hepburn as King Henry II and Queen Eleanor of Aquitaine, or more recent films like *Elizabeth* with Cate Blanchett as Queen Elizabeth I.

Since British history is inextricably linked to the personalities of its rulers throughout the centuries, *Royal London In Context* focuses on London's royal past as it explores the areas around the Houses of Parliament and Westminster Abbey, Whitehall, Horse Guards Parade, Trafalgar Square, Piccadilly, and St. James's Palace, and ends at Buckingham Palace, the London residence of Queen Elizabeth II. Along the way you will hear fascinating stories about the Royal Family and their roles in British history.

The *Europe In Context* series is designed for independent travelers who want to travel on their own schedule, while making the most of their precious vacation time. I have always preferred wandering about on my own, taking time to absorb the wonderful experience of overseas travel. I have never liked being herded, rushed, or told I have to wait until the 2 o'clock tour to begin my exploration of a new city. My heart has gone out to every fellow traveler who has had to strain to hear and understand the tour guide's canned spiel, or who has had to struggle to keep up with a fast-moving tour group as it tries to keep to its schedule. I have found the pre-recorded narration on the popular London bus tours lacks the depth and quality that I expect on my travels. I have taken innumerable individually guided tours offered by museums and city travel agencies, where I have had both wonderful and mediocre tour guides. It's simply a matter of chance. Using your personal CD player, *Royal London In Context* frees you from crowded tour groups and ensures a high-quality and engaging narration that will enrich your vacation experience, while allowing you to explore Royal London at your own pace. I hope you enjoy the independence it offers.

The Palace of Westminster, seat of the British Houses of Parliament.

Earth has not anything to show more fair:
Dull would he be of soul who could pass by
A sight so touching in its majesty;
This City now doth, like a garment, wear
The beauty of the morning; silent, bare,
Ships, towers, domes, theaters, and temples lie
Open unto the fields, and to the sky;
All bright and glittering in the smokeless air.
Never did sun more beautifully steep
In his first splendor, valley, rock, or hill;
Ne'er saw I, never felt, a calm so deep!
The river glideth at his own sweet will;
Dear God! the very houses seem asleep;
And all that mighty heart is lying still!

William Wordsworth (1770-1850)
"Sonnet Composed upon Westminster Bridge"
September 3, 1802

CONTENTS

INTRODUCTION:
HOW TO USE YOUR AUDIO CD GUIDE

There are probably more tour books written about London than any other destination in the world. London is filled with statues, memorials, royal palaces, and countless places of historical interest. *Royal London In Context* differs from all other guides to London in both its focus and format. The guide comes with two audio CDs filled with stories about the lives of Britain's kings, queens, and important historical figures that will bring to life the rich history of this extraordinary city.

The first chapter of this guide, "Description of the Twelve Tours," gives a brief overview of the highlights you will see on the twelve narrated tours offered on the two CDs included with your guide. The written guide has maps of the areas explored on each tour; a detailed diagram of the Houses of Parliament; and many photographs of the places and works discussed on the tours. The twelve tours are arranged in a natural, geographical sequence. You may explore London in the order of the tours presented, or you may skip to a track that deals with a site of particular interest to you. The sites selected for these twelve tours, as well as the specific monuments and works of art discussed, were carefully chosen to present an enjoyable and informative portrait of London's rich history. Presenting these tours in an Audio CD format allows you to pause in midplay during the tour narration to linger and admire a particular monument

or work of art that intrigues you; to examine something nearby that catches your attention; or to take a break in a neighborhood pub. Audio CD players permit you to pause or stop the play in mid-track. When you turn the CD player back on and push the play button, the track resumes playing at the point where you stopped. For the best results, use a newer sports model CD player with anti-skip protection to prevent your movements from jarring the CD play while you walk. If you use a "T-jack" and a second set of earphones, a couple traveling together can share one CD player and enjoy the narration at the same time. T-jacks

Queen Elizabeth II rides to the State Opening of Parliament.

The gates of Windsor Castle.

Tower Bridge.

are readily available at your local electronics or audio store.

The twelve narrated tours can be found on the two CDs included with this guide. Each narrated tour is on a separate track just like the track of a song on a music CD. For your convenience, the number of the tour corresponds to the track number on each CD. Tours 1 through 6 will be found on tracks 1 though 6 of CD One. Tours 7 through 12 will be found on tracks 7 through 12 of CD Two. At the beginning of CD Two, there are six tracks with about six seconds of silence on each track, so that the first narrated track containing Tour 7 begins on Track 7 of CD Two.

Directions for finding the physical starting point for each of the tours are given by the narrator at the beginning of each CD track. The beginning point for each of the twelve tours is also marked with the corresponding tour number circled in red, which you will find on the useful maps of the areas visited on the tours.

While you are enjoying your CD audio tours, at certain points during the narration on each track, we will suggest that you press the pause or stop button on your CD player to allow time for you to move to the next subject described. Pause or stop your CD player when you hear the musical cue identified in the narrated introduction on Track 1. Then push the play button on your CD player and resume the guide when you reach the next point identified in the narration. At the conclusion of each track, you will hear a different musical cue indicating the end of the segment, so that you can stop the CD player until you have reached the starting point for the tour covered on the next track.

Admiralty Arch leading to Buckingham Palace.　　Old Palace Yard of Westminster.

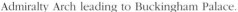

The tours in this guide will take you through some of the most popular and traffic-congested areas of London. Crossing streets in London can be tricky for the first-time visitor unfamiliar with cars driving on the left side of the street. So be very careful. When you come to a street crossing while taking any tour, remember to always push the pause or stop button on your CD player and take off your CD earphones. Look both ways before you cross the street and always cross at the designated crosswalks. When you push the play button, the CD player will pick up the narration exactly where you left off.

Chapter 2, "A History of the British Kings and Queens," provides an overview of Britain's royal history and explains how the role of the monarchy has changed over the centuries. It is recommended that you read this section before you begin your audio tours to become more familiar with British history. This will enhance your enjoyment of the narration provided in the tours.

Chapter 3, "The Role of the Monarchy—What Does the Queen Do?" looks at the role of the Queen in Britain's system of constitutional monarchy and parliamentary democracy; discusses the truth about the Queen's wealth; and examines the symbols of Royal Office and the Crown Jewels.

Chapter 4, "A Primer On Royalty, the Peerage and Titles of Nobility, Honours and the Orders of Chivalry," gives you the ABCs of royalty—accession, succession, and coronation, peerage and the different titles of nobility, and explains the different honors and orders of chivalry bestowed by the monarch at ceremonial investitures.

Chapter 5, "Planning Your Trip—Experiencing Royal London," provides in-depth information about the opportunities you have to experience royalty on display during your visit, including the famous Changing of the Guard, the Queen's Gallery, the Royal Mews, the Ceremony of the Keys, Westminster Abbey, the State Opening of Parliament, visiting the Houses of Parliament, Trooping the Color, Beating Retreat, Remembrance Sunday, and the Royal Gun Salutes.

Members of the Royal Household Guard.

Chapter 6, "The Royal Palaces and Fortresses," provides important historical background information, suggestions for planning your visit, and detailed information on how you can use public transportation to reach the important royal sites of Buckingham Palace, the Tower of London, Windsor Castle, Hampton Court, Kensington Palace, and Greenwich Palace.

Chapter 7, "Getting around London," provides comprehensive, practical information and clear instructions on how you can use London's convenient public transportation, including its Underground system, buses, light rail, trains, taxis, and riverboats to tour the city and to reach the royal sites on your own.

Chapter 8, "Arriving in London," offers information for visitors arriving by air and discusses your various options for getting to and from London's two principal airports, Gatwick and Heathrow.

Houses of Parliament viewed from the London Eye.

CHAPTER 1

DESCRIPTION OF THE TWELVE TOURS

TOUR 1
(CD One Track 1)

INTRODUCTION AND TOUR OF WESTMINSTER BRIDGE, STATUE OF QUEEN BOUDICCA, EXTERIOR OF THE HOUSES OF PARLIAMENT, BIG BEN, AND STATUE OF WINSTON CHURCHILL

"Among the noble cities of the world that are celebrated by Fame,
the City of London, seat of the Monarchy of England, is one that spreads
its fame wider, sends its wealth further,
and lifts its head higher than all the others."

William FitzStephen
(clerk to Thomas Becket, Archbishop of Canterbury)

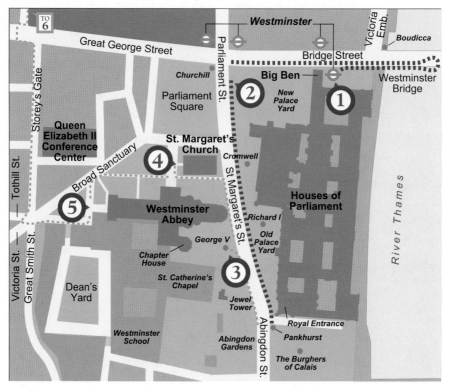

The red circled numbers above identify the starting points for each of the numbered tours. The square green box indicates the way to the starting point for the next tour.

The first tour, found on Track 1 of CD One, begins at the foot of Westminster Bridge standing beside the famous Houses of Parliament. To get there by the Underground system you can use the Jubilee, District, or Circle Lines. Get off at the Westminster Tube station. Take Exit #3, which will put you out at the north end of Westminster Bridge near the corner of the Houses of Parliament, where your tour begins. When you exit up the stairs, look for the elaborate lamp pole, which you will find to your right, where the narration begins.

On the opposite side of the street near Westminster Bridge stands the bronze statue of Boudicca, the 1st-century Celtic Queen of the Iceni, driving her war chariot with her spear held high. Hear the story of this remarkable warrior-queen. Learn why she rallied her people to rise up against the Roman conquerors, and left the Roman city of Londinium in ashes before she took her own life.

Stroll up to the middle of Westminster Bridge for an unforgettable Thames-eye view of the stately Palace of Westminster—home of the British Houses of Parliament. Listen as the narrator explains how England's Saxon King Edward the Confessor brought his court here

Queen Boudicca by Thomas Thornycroft.

by the river to build his Royal Palace beside Westminster Abbey. Discover how careless custodians started a devastating fire that destroyed Edward's medieval palace and how the building you see today came to be constructed in the mid-19th century in the Victorian Gothic style. You will be quite surprised to learn the different fates enjoyed by the new palace's two architects, Charles Barry and Augustus Welby Pugin.

Turn for a moment and stand with your back to the Palace of Westminster. Look across the River Thames as the narrator identifies nearby points of interest. The towering observation wheel known as the "London Eye" rises in front of the old County Hall to your left. On the other side of the bridge, you can see the red-bricked façade of St. Thomas's Hospital across the Thames from the Houses of Parliament. Hear the story of Florence Nightingale, known as the "Lady of the Lamp," who tended wounded British soldiers during the bloody Crimean War and then went on to establish Britain's first school of nursing.

The tour continues as you retrace your steps back to the foot of Westminster Bridge to take a closer look at perhaps

London Eye in front of the old County Hall.

15

the most recognizable sight in London—Big Ben. Learn how the bell of the famous clock tower got its name and how the tower narrowly survived the devastating Nazi bombardment that destroyed the House of Commons.

London's famed Big Ben.

Next, walk away from the River Thames, past Big Ben and along New Palace Yard, until you reach the corner of Westminster Bridge Street and Parliament Street, where the first tour concludes. Pause at the busy intersection and look across Parliament Square to admire the bronze statue of Sir Winston Churchill, who seems to glower back at the Houses of Parliament. Hear about the life of this towering figure, who courageously led the people of Britain through the darkest days of WWII but was voted out of office just after the Allies' victory over Nazi Germany. Learn how the nation later paid a final tribute to the great man as his body lay in state in Westminster Hall (located behind you).

Now turn to your left at the corner and continue walking down St. Margaret's Street. The next tour begins once you pass the gated entrance to New Palace Yard, where you will enjoy a side view of the legendary Westminster Hall and the narration for the next tour begins.

The statue of Sir Winston Churchill by Ivor Robert-Jones in Parliament Square.

T O U R   2
(CD One Track 2)

Tour of exterior of Westminster Hall, Statues of Oliver Cromwell and Richard I, Old Palace Yard, Victoria Tower Gardens, and Statue of Emmeline Pankhurst

"Those who imagine that a politician
would make a better figurehead than a hereditary monarch
might perhaps make the acquaintance of more politicians."

Baroness Margaret Thatcher,
Prime Minister 1979 - 1990

The second tour, found on Track 2 of CD One, begins standing beside the venerable Westminster Hall. (See map on page 14.) Listen as the narrator recounts the colorful past of this marvel of medieval engineering. It was once the site of lavish court celebrations and dramatic trials, including the trials of Scottish rebel leader William Wallace of *Braveheart* fame, Henry VIII's former Lord Chancellor Sir Thomas More, and King Charles I, who was condemned to death here at Westminster Hall after being deposed in the English Civil War. Learn about the surprising discovery recently made by workmen concerning Henry VIII's use of the huge hall for more playful royal pursuits.

Proceed further down St. Margaret's Street to stand in front of the statue of Oliver Cromwell—the controversial leader in the English Civil War. The statue stands beside Westminster Hall on a platform with a bronze lion at its base. Learn how Cromwell led Parliamentary forces to overthrow King Charles I, ushering in Puritan rule, only to have Cromwell become a virtual dictator. You will be amazed to learn that even the celebration of Christmas was banned by the religious conservatives, who supported Cromwell's iron rule as Lord Protector. Listen as the narrator describes the grisly revenge carried out against Cromwell when the monarchy was restored under Charles II.

Oliver Cromwell by H. Thornycroft.

Richard the Lion-Heart by C. Marochetti.

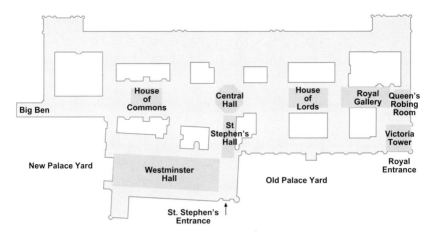

Walk down the sidewalk past St. Stephen's Entrance to the House of Commons until you stand in front of the equestrian statue of Richard I, known as Richard the Lion-Heart—the subject of countless colorful tales and heroic legends. Listen as the narrator recounts the true-life story behind this famous warrior-king.

The area around the statue of Richard I and to your right is called Old Palace Yard, because it was once the courtyard of the old Palace of Westminster. Learn of the secret pro-Catholic plans in 1605 to kill King James I in the famous Gunpowder Plot and how, when the deadly scheme was uncovered, Guy Fawkes was found—a few feet from where you are standing—with 30 barrels of gunpowder ready to blow up Parliament.

The tour continues as you walk away from the statue of Richard I. Proceed along the sidewalk until you reach the Sovereign's Entrance to the House of Lords, where stone lions stand guard on either side of the magnificent doorway. Listen as the narrator explains the splendid ceremony of the State Opening of Parliament, where the Queen rides in the Irish State Coach in a grand procession from Buckingham Palace, escorted by bands and the mounted cavalry of the Household Division, and enters through these doors to address the assembled crowd of Lords and

Side view of Westminster Hall.

Regal Lion beside the Royal Entrance.

Emmeline Pankhurst by A.G. Walker.

Members of Parliament. (For more information about this glittering royal event, see page 131.)

Resume your walk down the sidewalk away from the statue of Richard I until you reach the entrance to the Victoria Tower Gardens. The second tour concludes just inside the shady garden. On the left as you enter you will see the statue of Emmeline Pankhurst. Learn of her role in the tumultuous suffragette movement and hear how the decades-long struggle eventually gave women the right to vote. At the conclusion of your tour you may wish to take a break and stroll through the pleasant Victoria Tower Gardens. Enjoy the lovely views across the Thames and be sure to see the remarkable bronze sculptural group—a copy of Auguste Rodin's *The Burghers of Calais*—depicting the city leaders of Calais who surrendered as hostages to save their city from destruction by King Edward III in 1347. (For more information about visiting the Houses of Parliament, see page 132.)

Rodin's *The Burghers of Calais*.

TOUR 3
(CD One Track 3)

TOUR OF STATUE OF GEORGE V, EXTERIORS OF THE HENRY VII CHAPEL OF WESTMINSTER ABBEY, AND THE JEWEL TOWER

"Being a nation of hypocrites, we have for years looked to the Royal Family to embody the values we're not prepared to embody ourselves."

Serena Mackesy,
The Independent, December 10, 1996

The third tour, found on Track 3 of CD One, begins at the statue of George V, which stands on a tall, white pedestal in the small park beside the east end of Westminster Abbey. (See map on page 14.) Cross the street at the marked crosswalk and walk over to admire the dignified statue of King George V—a pivotal figure in Britain's royal past. Hear about the life of the grandson of Queen Victoria, who ruled Britain through the turbulence of World War I and the Great Depression. Learn about the family ties that led to bitter resentment against the King and a name change for the Royal Family, the fateful political decision that haunted the King for the rest of his life, and the long-hushed-up circumstances surrounding the beloved King's death. Listen as the narrator describes how George V's eldest son, faced with pressure from the Royal Family, the Archbishop of Canterbury, and his own Prime Minister, renounced his claim to the throne rather than give up the woman he loved, and how his painfully shy younger brother unexpectedly assumed the crown. Learn how the introverted King George VI, with the help of his loving wife, rose to meet the challenges of kingship and united the people of Britain during the difficult times of WWII.

See where England took its first cautious steps towards representative government following the rebellion against Henry III in the 13th century and where William Caxton set up England's first printing press and published a collection of stories called the *Canterbury Tales*, written by a former clerk at Westminster Abbey, Geoffrey Chaucer. The tour concludes as you walk over to observe a remnant of the old Palace of Westminster that survived the devastating 1834 fire—the Jewel Tower, built by King Edward III in 1366 to house his Royal Treasury.

George V by William Reid Dick and Giles Gilbert Scott.

Jewel Tower

Admission charge; Open daily April 1 - September 30: 10:00 a.m. - 6:00 p.m.; October 1 - October 31: 10:00 a.m.- 5:00 p.m.; November 1 - March 31: 10:00 a.m. - 4:00 p.m. (closed December 24-26, January 1).

TOUR 4
(CD One Track 4)

TOUR OF THE INTERIOR OF
ST. MARGARET'S CHURCH AND
EXTERIOR OF WESTMINSTER ABBEY

"To be a king and wear a crown
is more glorious to them that see it
than it is a pleasure to them that bear it."

Queen Elizabeth I

The fourth tour, found on Track 4 of CD One, begins in front of St. Margaret's Church, near the main entrance to Westminster Abbey. (See map on page 14.) Learn about the fascinating history of this small parish church, which stands in the shadow of its more famous neighbor—Westminster Abbey. The tour continues inside St. Margaret's Church where you will see the stunning stained glass windows commissioned to celebrate the wedding of Catherine of Aragon and Prince Arthur, elder son and heir apparent of Henry VII. By the time the beautiful windows arrived, Arthur had died, and the young Henry VIII had entered into the ill-fated marriage with his brother's widow. Learn how their bitter divorce changed the face of England forever and led to centuries of deadly religious strife. Beside the high altar is the resting place of the headless body of Sir Walter Raleigh. Hear the strange story of the death of the explorer and onetime courtier to Queen Elizabeth I who lost his head under Elizabeth's successor, King James I.

St. Margaret's Church

Admission is free, donations accepted; Open Monday - Friday 9:30 a.m. – 3:45 p.m.; Saturday 9:30 a.m. – 1:45 p.m.; Sunday 2:00 p.m. – 5:00 p.m. Church may be closed for special services and other events. For more information, check its Web site, www.westminster-abbey.org/stmargarets.

The tour continues outside the front of St. Margaret's Church, near the main entrance to the abbey, where you will find another telltale reminder of London's ancient Roman past. Listen as the narrator describes the origins of the abbey and recounts the legend of why the pious King Edward the Confessor devoted his reign to the building of this great abbey church dedicated to St. Peter. (For more information on the history of the abbey, and suggestions for planning your visit, see page 129.)

Westminster Abbey

Admission charge; Open Monday - Friday 9:30 a.m. - 4:45 p.m. (last admission 3:45 p.m.); Wednesday evening second session 6:00 p.m. - 7:00 p.m.; Saturday 9:30 a.m. - 2:45 p.m. (last admission 1:45 p.m.); Sunday the abbey is only open for worship services. For more information, check its Web site, www.westminster-abbey.org.

North entrance to Westminster Abbey.

TOUR 5
(CD One Track 5)

TOUR OF THE EXTERIOR OF THE GREAT WESTERN PORTAL OF WESTMINSTER ABBEY AND BROAD SANCTUARY

"The Queen's appearances abroad do more
in a day to gain goodwill for Britain than all the politicians
and diplomats lumped together could achieve in years."

Sir Alec Douglas-Home,
Prime Minister 1963 - 1964

Queen Elizabeth by J.P. Philips.

Great West Portal of Westminster.

The fifth tour, found on Track 5 of CD One, begins at the gated exit just outside the Great West Portal of Westminster Abbey. (See map on page 14.) Above the exit doors you will see the latest addition to the abbey—ten statues honoring 20th century Christian martyrs, including the familiar figure of civil rights leader Dr. Martin Luther King, Jr. To the right of the statues and above the Westminster Bookstore, you will see the rooftop of Westminster's Jerusalem Chapel. Find out how Bible scholars gathered here during the reign of James I to carry out their historic task of revising the English translation of the Bible.

The area stretching along the side of the abbey and near the Great West Portal is known as Broad Sanctuary. This is where medieval refugees could claim the right of sanctuary with the monks of the abbey and escape the king's justice. Listen as the narrator describes the dramatic standoff that took place here in the 15th century that ended when the young boys, known in legend as "the Little Princes," were sent to the Tower of London by their uncle Richard, Duke of Gloucester, never to be seen again.

Next, stand with your back to the Great West Portal and admire the tall, red granite column which commemorates the soldiers known as the "old boys of Westminster School" who lost their lives in the 1853 Crimean War and the 1857 Indian Mutiny. Before moving on to the next tour, take a peek through the arched Gothic gateway to your left to see inside the courtyard of the famous Westminster School, founded by Queen Elizabeth I.

T O U R 6
(CD One Track 6)

TOUR OF EXTERIOR OF THE OLD CABINET WAR ROOMS, STATUE OF ROBERT CLIVE, THE CENOTAPH, AND No. 10 DOWNING STREET

"The Crown has become the mysterious link,
may I say the magic link, which unites our loosely bound,
but strongly interwoven Commonwealth of Nations, states and races.
People who would never tolerate the assertions of a written
Constitution, which implies any diminution of their independence
are the foremost to be proud of their loyalty to the Crown."

Winston Churchill,
Prime Minister, 1940 - 1945 and 1951 - 1955

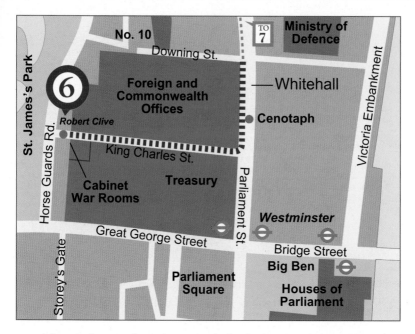

The sixth tour, found on Track 6 of CD One, begins near the stairs leading to King Charles Street, where you will see the statue of Robert Clive. To reach the starting point for the sixth tour from the ending point of Tour No. 5, walk away from the Great West Portal of Westminster Abbey until you reach the crosswalk, which will take you over Victoria Street. (See the route marked in green on the map on page 14.) Bear right and cross Tothill Street, where you will pass in front of the Methodist Central Hall to Storey's Gate. Walk down Storey's Gate, which will lead you behind the ultramodern Queen Elizabeth II Conference Center, and which ends at Great George Street. When you reach the end of Storey's Gate, turn left, and walk a few paces down Great George Street. Go to the crosswalk over Great George Street. Turn right at the corner and cross Horse Guards Road. Then turn left and walk along Horse Guards Road to the stairs beside the statue of Robert Clive.

If you are beginning your sightseeing with Tour No. 6, you can reach the starting point by using the Jubilee, District, or Circle Lines to take you to the Westminster Tube station. Take Exit #5, which will put you out at the corner of Parliament Street and Great George Street across from Parliament Square. Turn right and walk away from Parliament Square one block up Parliament Street (which becomes Whitehall) to King Charles Street. Turn left onto King Charles Street, passing under the arch, and go down the pedestrian street towards Horse Guards Road and St. James's Park, which you will see in the distance. Walk to the end. Go down the stairs and stand in front of the statue of Robert Clive, where the sixth tour's narration begins.

To the right of the stairs you will see a curious, sandbagged doorway. This was the entrance to the secret, fortified basement where Winston Churchill met with his wartime ministers during World War II. The very existence of this top-secret location was not disclosed until 1981 when Prime Minister Margaret Thatcher decided that the historic site should become a national museum. Listen as the narrator describes the harrowing tale of how Churchill and his top advisers huddled together in this claustrophobic underground warren of rooms to plot the defense of Britain as bombs rained down on London during the German bombing campaign known as the Blitz.

Cabinet War Rooms and Churchill Museum

Admission charge; Open daily October 1 - March 31: 10:00 a.m. - 6:00 p.m. (last admission 5:15 p.m.); April 1 – September 30: 9:30 a.m. - 6:00 p.m. (last admission 5:15 p.m.). The Museum is part of the British Imperial War Museum. For more information, check its Web site, www.iwm.org.uk/cabinet.

Climb the stairs to stand beside the statue of Robert Clive, known as the "Conqueror of India." Learn how this lowly clerk in the East India Company became a successful commander in the military arm of the company. He brought India into the British Empire, while amassing personal wealth and a title. However, he was later brought down by financial scandal and ended his life in a suicide.

The tour continues as you walk towards Parliament Street. Pass under the decorative archway over the end of King Charles Street and turn left onto Parliament Street, which becomes Whitehall. In the center of Whitehall you will see the austere, white memorial erected to honor the British and

Entrance to the Cabinet War Rooms Museum.

Commonwealth soldiers and citizens who lost their lives during the First and Second World Wars. Listen as the narrator describes how the memorial was dedicated and how each year on Remembrance Sunday, the Sunday nearest to the 11th of November, the Queen leads the whole nation in solemn tribute to all those who have given their lives in defense of the United Kingdom and the Commonwealth. (For more information on attending this solemn event, see page 136.)

Sir Edwin Lutyen's Cenotaph.

Continue up Whitehall away from King Charles Street until you reach No. 10 Downing Street, where this tour concludes at the well-guarded entrance to Downing Street and the homes of the British Prime Minister, the Chancellor of the Exchequer, and the Party Whip. You will be astonished to hear the fascinating story behind the origins of this famous street. Learn the surprising twist in the tale of how a young Harvard graduate was rewarded when he returned to England to join the fight to overthrow Charles I and rose to become Cromwell's chief spy, only to be rewarded again when he switched sides to restore the monarchy.

You will discover how the role of the Prime Minister first began when England's new king, George I, could not speak English! The next tour begins just up Whitehall at the Horse Guards building. Continue walking up Whitehall. You will pass the Cabinet Offices and then the Scottish Office on your left before you reach the mounted sentries at the gates of the Horse Guards building, where narration for the next tour begins.

TOUR 7
(CD Two Track 7)

TOUR OF HORSE GUARD PARADE, EXTERIORS OF THE BANQUETING HOUSE, GREAT SCOTLAND YARD, AND THE OLD ADMIRALTY

"I think it is a misconception to imagine that the monarchy
exists in the interests of the monarch. It doesn't.
It exists in the interests of the people."

HRH Prince Philip, Duke of Edinburgh

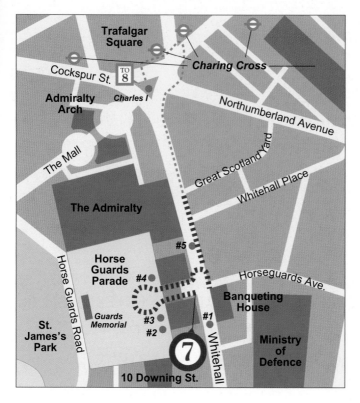

#1 Statue of Douglas, first Earl Haig (Commander of British forces in WWI)
#2 Cadiz Memorial (given by Spain for Wellington's help in lifting Napoleon's siege of Cadiz)
#3 Statue of Garnet Joseph, first Viscount Wolseley (prototype of "Modern Major-General" character in *The Pirates of Penzance*)
#4 Statue of Frederick Sleigh, first Earl Roberts (hero of the Boer and Afghan Wars)
#5 Statue of the second Duke of Clarence, (Commander-in-Chief of British Armed Forces 1865 - 1895)

The seventh tour, found on Track 7 of CD Two, begins on Whitehall standing before the 18th-century Horse Guards building. Each day from 10:00 a.m. until 4:00 p.m., two mounted sentries stand guard on either side. The sentries and their beautiful horses stoically endure their one-hour tour of duty as crowds of tourists line up to pose for their souvenir photographs. Until 1841, this was the main entrance to St. James's and Buckingham Palaces. It was built on the site where the old guardhouse of Henry VIII's Whitehall Palace once stood. Today the building is home to the Queen's two Household Cavalry mounted regiments—the Life Guards and the Blues and Royals, which were formed during the Restoration of the Monarchy under King Charles II to protect the Royal Family. Today the Household Cavalry regiments provide escort for the monarch on all ceremonial and state occasions.

Enter into the front courtyard and walk under the center archway to Horse Guards Parade, which leads to St. James's Park on the other side. Find out about the history of Horse Guards Parade, which was once the tilting yard for colorful tournaments and jousts during the time of Henry VIII. Now it's the site for the elaborate annual military spectacle known as "Trooping the Color," celebrating the Queen's official birthday. (For more information about the history of this colorful martial pageant and to learn how you can plan to attend the ceremony, see page 133.)

William Kent's Horse Guards Parade building.

Take a moment to explore Horse Guards Parade grounds before returning through the archway back to Whitehall.

The tour continues back on Whitehall. After you exit through the forecourt of the Horse Guards building, pass through the gates, and turn left onto Whitehall. Once you pass the mounted sentry, stand for a moment and look across Whitehall. To the right, you will observe the exterior of the Banqueting House—a revolutionary design by Inigo Jones that changed the course of English architecture. Cross Whitehall at the marked crosswalk. Turn right and walk back down Whitehall past the intersection of Horseguards Avenue to the gated entrance to the Banqueting House. Learn about the history of Whitehall Palace and find out how the high and mighty Cardinal Wolsey fell from royal grace when he failed to win the Pope's permission for Henry VIII's divorce; losing his palaces and possessions. Wolsey died on the way to face the King's wrath.

The Banqueting House was the scene of one of the most dramatic events in England's history—the public execution of King

Mounted sentry of the Life Guards.

The Cadiz Memorial—a French mortar mounted on a Chinese dragon.

The Guards Memorial.

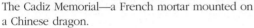

Charles I. Listen as the narrator recounts how the doomed King, deposed by Cromwell's forces, stepped out through a second-story window in the building you see before you onto the scaffold to his execution on that cold afternoon of January 30, 1649.

Look up above the entrance to the top of the Banqueting House. Discover the secret of the weather vane placed there by Charles II's brother and successor, James II, so he could check each morning to see if a "Protestant wind" was blowing from Holland that would bring his son-in-law, the Protestant Prince William of Orange, and the King's daughter Mary to the throne to prevent England's return to Catholicism. You won't believe how false rumors of a healthy baby boy being secretly smuggled into the palace in a warming pan led to the overthrow of James II in the Glorious Revolution of 1688.

Banqueting House

Admission charge; Open Monday – Saturday 10:00 a.m. – 5:00. p.m. (closed Sunday, official holidays, December 24 – January 1). Use of an audiotape guide is included in the price of admission. A short film on the history of the building is shown continuously in the Undercroft.

The tour continues as you turn away from the Banqueting House and walk up Whitehall. You will again cross over Horseguards Avenue and then Whitehall Place. Resume the Guide when you reach the corner of Whitehall

Horse Guards Parade—the venue for the annual Trooping the Color.

and Great Scotland Yard, where the narrative continues. A pub now stands on this famous corner, but at one time the mansion used by the Scottish Kings and their ambassadors was located nearby. Learn how London's first organized police force got its name from that mansion and how London's police officers came to be called "Bobbies."

Turn and stand with your back to Great Scotland Yard, and look across the street to see the walled entrance to the Old Admiralty building—home of the powerful British Navy that ruled the waves during the last half of the 19th century. Hear the story of how the death of Lord Nelson in the fateful naval Battle of Trafalgar on October 21, 1805, plunged the nation into mourning. You might be surprised to hear how Lord Nelson's body was preserved by his resourceful officers until

Inigo Jones's Banqueting House.

The perfect double cube interior of Inigo Jones's Banqueting House.

The corner of Whitehall and Great Scotland Yard—now a popular pub.

his remains were brought here to lie in state at the Old Admiralty building on January 8, 1806.

The next tour begins further up the street, where Whitehall ends at Trafalgar Square. Cross the street at the marked crosswalk and then walk over to the equestrian statue of Charles I on the small plaza at the south end of Trafalgar Square, where the narration for the next tour begins.

The second Duke of Clarence, Commander-in-Chief of British Armed Forces 1865 - 1895.

TOUR 8
(CD Two Track 8)

TOUR OF TRAFALGAR SQUARE, STATUE OF CHARLES I, NELSON'S COLUMN, STATUES OF SIR HENRY HAVELOCK AND GEORGE IV, EXTERIOR OF THE CHURCH OF ST. MARTIN-IN-THE-FIELDS

"Why, Sir, you find no man, at all intellectual,
who is willing to leave London.
No, Sir, when a man is tired of London, he is tired of life;
for there is in London all that life can afford."

James Boswell, *The Life of Samuel Johnson*

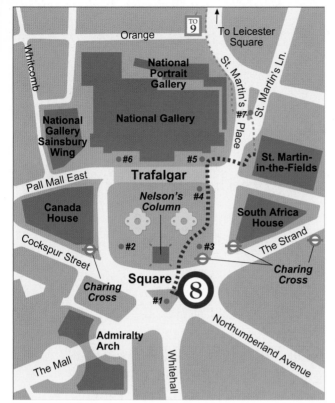

#1 Statue of Charles I
#2 Statue of Gen. Sir Charles Napier
#3 Statue of Sir Henry Havelock
#4 Statue of George IV
#5 Statue of George Washington
#6 Statue of James II
#7 Statue of Nurse Edith Cavell

The eighth tour, found on Track 8 of CD Two, begins on the small pedestrian plaza located just south of Trafalgar Square by the equestrian statue of Charles I. The nearest Tube stations are Charing Cross, which serves the Northern and Bakerloo Lines, and Leicester Square, which serves the Northern and Piccadilly Lines.

The elegant figure of Charles I looks down Whitehall towards the Banqueting House, where the King was executed by Cromwell's forces. Hear how an enterprising metal worker hoodwinked both Cromwell and the Royalists and made a fortune secretly selling bits of the supposedly destroyed statue to supporters of the fallen King. He was pardoned when the long-lost statue was "miraculously restored" and presented to the King's son, Charles II. You will be touched by the story of Edward I, who was so grief-stricken at the death of his wife, Queen Eleanor of Castile, that he erected memorial crosses at each stop made in her solemn funeral procession to Westminster Abbey. The last and largest of the "Eleanor Crosses" stood on this site and was called Charing Cross. A Victorian replica stands outside

Charing Cross Train Station.

Facing the front of the statue of Charles I, turn and look to your left. You will see the curving façade of the Admiralty Arch, which was designed as a part of the grand ceremonial processional route constructed by Sir Aston Webb in 1911. It was built at the request of King Edward VII in honor of his mother, Queen Victoria, and was finally completed at

(above) Playful fountains by Charles Wheeler and W. McMillan. *(below)* One of Trafalgar Square's familiar bronze lions by Edwin Landseer.

the beginning of the reign of her grandson, George V.

Now cross the street to explore Trafalgar Square. The square, designed by Sir Charles Barry—famous for the Houses of Parliament—was built to commemorate Lord Nelson's celebrated victory in the Battle of Trafalgar. Listen as the narrator describes the story behind Lord Nelson's imposing Column and the creation of the lovable bronze lions, which were later added around its base. You will be disappointed to learn how the staid British government ignored the last wishes of the nation's fallen naval hero and allowed Nelson's beloved mistress to die in poverty.

The narrator will tell you about the history of this beautiful square and the important buildings surrounding London's favorite gathering place. The tour continues as you examine the statue of Sir Henry Havelock and learn what pioneering 19th century technological innovation was used in its creation. Then walk up past Havelock's statue to the right of Edwin Lutyens' cloverleaf fountains until you reach the equestrian statue of extravagant King George IV. Take a seat on the nearby benches and listen as the narrator recounts the tales of one of Britain's

George IV by Francis Leggatt Chantrey.

least glorious rulers, whose vanity helped shape the face of the London we see today.

Proceed up the stairs to the North Terrace, where you will reach the front of the world-renowned British National Gallery. Built in 1838, the museum houses one of the greatest collections of European paintings in the world, with over 2,300 works from the 13th through the 20th centuries. Nearby, on the lawn in front of the Gallery, you will see the bronze statue of George Washington sculpted by the 18th-century French artist Jean-Antoine Houdon. Further down, you will see the bronze statue of James II by Grinling Gibbons.

To the right of the National Gallery stands a graceful church with its tall, impressive spire. Cross over the busy street to the famed church of St. Martin-in-the-Fields, which was designed by the Scottish architect James Gibbs, a student of Christopher Wren. Walk up the steps to the portico of the church, where you will find the strikingly modern sculpture *In The*

Beginning by Mike Chapman. Pause and listen to the history of this proud church, rightly famous for its commitment to social activism and its rich musical tradition. You might wish to take a break and visit the National Gallery or the National Portrait Gallery, which is located just a block further up the street, or enjoy a break in the wonderful Café in the Crypt of St. Martin-in-the-Fields. The next tour begins at Piccadilly Circus near the statue of the winged Angel known as "Eros."

St. Martin-in-the-Fields.

National Gallery

Admission free (charge for special exhibitions); Open daily 10:00 a.m. - 6:00 p.m.; Wednesday evenings until 9:00 p.m. (closed December 24-26, January 1). For information on its current exhibitions, check its Web site, www. national-gallery.org.uk.

St. Martin-in-the-Fields

Admission free; Open Monday - Saturday 9:00 a.m. - 6:00 p.m.; Sundays 11:30 a.m. - 6:00 p.m. The church continues its tradition of music with a series of evening and lunchtime concerts. For a schedule of services and upcoming concerts, check its Web site, www.stmartin-in-the-fields.org. The Café in the Crypt offers a quiet respite from the jostling crowds of Trafalgar Square with quick and reasonably priced meals and snacks and clean restrooms. Open Monday - Wednesday 10:00 a.m. - 8:00 p.m.; Thursday - Saturday 10:00 a.m. - 11:00 p.m.; Sunday 12:00 p.m. - 8:00 p.m.

National Portrait Gallery

Admission free; Open daily Monday - Wednesday 10:00 a.m. - 6:00 p.m.; Thursday - Friday 10:00 a.m. - 9:00 p.m.; Saturday - Sunday 10:00 a.m. - 6:00 p.m. (closed Good Friday, December 24-26, January 1). The Museum offers a superb audio guide to the collection, which is available for a small fee. For information on its current exhibitions, check its Web site, www.npg.org.uk.

(top) Trafalgar Square at night. *(above)* View of Trafalgar Square's fountain and one of the famed bronze lions.

TOUR 9
(CD Two Track 9)

TOUR OF PICCADILLY CIRCUS, STATUE OF EROS, INTERIOR OF THE CHURCH OF ST. JAMES'S, JERMYN STREET, EXTERIORS OF FORTNUM AND MASON, THE ROYAL ACADEMY OF ARTS, AND THE BURLINGTON ARCADE

"London ... takes a lot of understanding. It's a great place. Immense.
The richest town in the world, the biggest port,
the greatest manufacturing town,
the Imperial city—the centre of civilization,
the heart of the world."

H. G. Wells

(left) Delightful figure of the *Angel of Christian Charity* by Sir Alfred Gilbert.

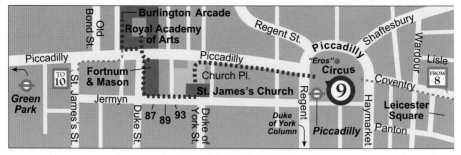

The ninth tour, found on Track 9 of CD Two, begins at Piccadilly Circus. The nearest Tube station is Piccadilly, which serves the Piccadilly and Bakerloo Lines. Look for the exit sign indicating the way to "Eros." The steps will lead you to the front of the statue. To reach the starting point for the ninth tour from the ending point of Tour No. 8, walk away from the Church of St. Martin-in-the-Fields and Trafalgar Square past the National Portrait Gallery on your left. (See map on page 38.) The street becomes Charing Cross Road. Continue on past Bear Street, which leads to Leicester Square. Turn left at the next street, Cranbourn, which turns into Coventry Street. It is poorly marked, but the Leicester Square Tube station will be on the opposite side of Charing Cross Road. Continue past the boisterous crowds of Leicester Square. Cross over Haymarket Street to reach Piccadilly Circus, where the narration for the ninth tour begins.

Situated at the junction of five major roads and lined with huge, glaring, neon signs, Piccadilly Circus is the Times Square of London. The area is bustling with activity as the gateway to London's non-stop entertainment district with theaters, restaurants, shops, pubs, and clubs. Learn how this lively area got its name from the fashionable creation of a 17th-century tailor who lived nearby. The centerpiece of Piccadilly Circus is the famous statue of the winged archer. The playful figure of the *Angel of Christian Charity* was erected as a memorial to the philanthropist Lord Shaftesbury, but became popularly known as "Eros"—the Greek God of carnal love. Listen as the narrator describes how the creation of this popular symbol of London became a nightmare for its creator, Sir Alfred Gilbert.

Begin your stroll down Piccadilly. Walk away from the statue. Pause at the corner of Piccadilly and Regent Street. Look to the left down Regent Street and listen to the tale of the second son of George III, the spendthrift Duke of York, whom you will see in the distance sitting atop the 124-foot-high column—high enough to be just out of reach of his many creditors. The tour continues as you proceed down Piccadilly for two blocks. The narration resumes when you reach the gated entrance to St. James's Church, which will be down on your left after you pass Church Place.

Learn how the grateful King Charles I rewarded his faithful supporter, Henry Jermyn, Earl of St. Albans, with a grant of land, which today is known as "St. James's." St. James's Church, designed by Sir Christopher Wren, was consecrated in 1684. It quickly became the parish church for the new aristocracy during the Restoration of the Monarchy.

Step into the churchyard. On the left of the main door you will see an unusual outdoor pulpit. To the right of the door you will see the quiet Garden of Remembrance dedicated to the Londoners who survived the terrors of the Blitz in World War II. In the garden you will find the modern Wren Café, which offers a great light lunch, refreshments, and clean restrooms. Today this progressive Anglican Church is known as the "Visitors Church."

Enter through the main church door beside the outdoor pulpit. Turn left into the church sanctuary and walk up the center aisle to admire the beautifully proportioned interior. St. James's was one of Wren's favorite churches. Inside you can admire the exquisite craftsmanship of Wren's master carver, Grinling Gibbons, in his magnificent altarpiece, organ case, and intricately carved marble baptismal font (found to the left of the entrance to the sanctuary).

St. James's Church

Admission free; Open daily 9:00 a.m.–6:00 p.m. For information, check its Web site, www.st-james-piccadilly.org. The church frequently hosts lunch recitals, lectures, and an evening concert series. For a schedule of upcoming events, check its Web site, www.stjamesconcerts.musicwise.net

Once you exit the sanctuary, turn left—opposite the direction you entered. Take the stairs down onto the street and turn right onto Jermyn Street. The shops in this posh area have catered to the upper classes since Henry Jermyn, Earl of St. Albans, developed the fields northeast of St. James's Palace into an elegant suburb

Elegant shop front of Floris, perfumery to the Queen.

Famed Royal Grocer Fortnum's.

for members of the court. Window-shop as you stroll down this stylish street. Learn about the Royal Warrants, which you will see over the doors of many of the shops along the way, including Floris, official perfumery to the British Royal Family.

When you reach Duke Street, turn right and return to Piccadilly to the entrance to the Queen's grocer—Fortnum and Mason. Listen as the narrator recounts the story of how William Fortnum, a footman in the service of Queen Anne, turned his royal connections into a successful business enterprise with his friend, Hugh Mason.

Turn and stand with your back to Fortnum's. Across the street and a bit to your left, you will see the Italianate arched entrance to the Burlington House. Cross to the other side of Piccadilly at the designated crosswalk. Pass under the archway into the courtyard of the Palladian-style former home of the Earl of Burlington, where you will learn about the Royal Academy of Arts, which was founded in 1768.

Royal Academy of Arts

Admission charge; Open daily 10:00 a.m. – 6:00 p.m. (until 10:00 p.m. Fridays). For a complete schedule of its current exhibitions, check its Web site, www.royalacademy.org.uk.

Return to Piccadilly and turn to the right. Step next door to the Burlington Arcade—one of the oldest covered shopping malls in the world—built by Lord George Cavendish in 1819. Enter the arcade and take a step back into the 19th century. Admire its beautifully carved mahogany shop fronts. Look for the Burlington Arcade security guards called "Beadles," decked out in their top hats and Edwardian frock coats, who patrol the arcade to ensure that shoppers uphold Lord Cavendish's strict rules of decorum.

The tenth tour begins at the corner of Piccadilly and St. James's. Exit Burlington Arcade and turn right. Cross over Piccadilly, returning back to the same side as Fortnum and Mason. Walk a block further down Piccadilly away from Fortnum and Mason and bear left around the corner of St. James's, where the narration for the next tour begins.

TOUR 10
(CD Two Track 10)

TOUR OF ST. JAMES'S STREET, EXTERIORS OF WHITE'S CLUB, LOBB & CO., LOCK & CO., PICKERING PLACE, BERRY BROTHERS AND RUDD, LTD., PALL MALL, EXTERIORS OF ST. JAMES'S PALACE, THE CHAPEL ROYAL AND THE QUEEN'S CHAPEL, QUEEN ALEXANDRA MEMORIAL, AND FRIARY COURT

"Oh, London is a famous town, A very famous city,
Where all the streets are paved with gold,
And all the maidens pretty."

George Colman the younger, 1797

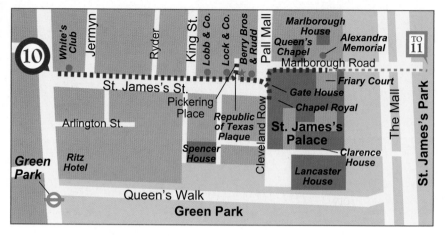

The tenth tour, found on Track 10 of CD Two, begins at the corner of Piccadilly and St. James's. The nearest Tube station is Green Park, which can be reached on the Piccadilly, Victoria, or Jubilee Lines. Exit using the "Piccadilly South" exit. Green Park will be on your right. Walk away from Green Park, past the fabulous Ritz Hotel. Cross over Arlington Street. Next you come to St. James's Street. Cross to the other side of St. James's Street and turn right.

The narration for the tour begins as you walk down this stylish street towards St. James's Palace. St. James's Street is lined with the most exclusive private gentlemen's clubs and shops of London. Pause at No. 37 St. James's, where you will learn about the oldest of London's gentlemen's clubs— White's, which was founded in 1693. Hear the story of Beau Brummell, the dandy who helped set the fashion trends of the "Regency"—named for his

patron, the future George IV. The tour continues as you walk downhill towards St. James's Palace. Cross over Ryder and King Streets. Pause again once you reach No. 9 St. James's. Peek in the window of Lobb and Company, and learn about the official

The bay window of the gentlemen's club, White's.

48

custom shoe and boot maker to the Royal Family. Further down at No. 6 St. James's you will come to Lock and Company Hatters—London's finest haberdashery since 1764. Hear the narrator describe the many innovations made by this small shop for its elite clientele.

After you pass the windows of Lock and Company, turn in the alleyway on your left called Pickering Place. You will be amused to discover the link between this quiet courtyard of 18th-century houses and the former Republic of Texas.

Return up to St. James's and turn left to admire the front windows of Berry Brothers and Rudd, Ltd., as you hear the story of how the small grocery store founded here in 1696 became the supplier of spirits to the British Royal Family. Pause at the corner of St. James's Street and Pall Mall. Discover how a popular game played by King Charles II gave its name to this wide avenue.

Continue on and cross at the designated crosswalk over to the tall Tudor gatehouse of St. James's Palace, which you will see to the right. This was the official London residence of the sovereign from 1698 until Queen Victoria moved into Buckingham Palace in 1837. Today, ambassadors to Britain from other countries are still formally accredited to the Court of St. James's. Walk past the gatehouse and see the large window of the Chapel Royal, as you learn how the palace

(top to bottom) Pickering Place, the elegant shop front of St. James's Lock & Co. Hatters, and Berry Bros. & Rudd, Ltd.

Tudor gatehouse of St. James's Palace.

was built here in the 1530's by Henry VIII on the site of the former convent and leper colony of St. James. Listen as the narrator recounts the intriguing stories of the many Royal events, both tragic and joyous, that have taken place behind these red brick walls.

Stroll along the palace exterior down Cleveland Row until you reach Stable Yard Road and learn how one lucky mistress of Charles II was rewarded for her services to the crown. On the left at the end of Cleveland Row is the gated entrance to Stable Yard Road. The entrance is now protected by a security gate and guards. On the right, you will see the Lancaster House, built in 1827 for the Duke of York. It is now used for state and diplomatic functions. On the left, you will see the white façade of Clarence House. It was built in 1825 by John Nash for the Duke of Clarence, the younger brother of George IV who later came to the throne as William IV.

Clarence House was the long-time home of Elizabeth Bowes-Lyon, mother of Queen Elizabeth II. The Queen Mother, affectionately known as the "Queen Mum," lived at Clarence House from 1953, when her daughter, came to the throne, until her death in 2002 at age 101. Clarence House is now the official London residence of Prince Charles (and his mistress, Camilla Parker-Bowles), and the Prince's sons, William and Harry. The

Side view of St. James's Palace.

five ground rooms used for public receptions are now open to the public by guided tour for a few weeks each year in the late summer.

Clarence House

Admission charge; Open August 6 - October 17: 9:00 a.m. - 7:00 p.m. All tickets are timed and must be booked in advance. For reservations: (0) 20 7766 7303; To purchase tickets on-line, go to www.the-royal-collection.com/royaltickets. E-mail: information@royalcollection.org.uk.

Nearby you will find Spencer House, the ancestral home of Diana, Princess of Wales. This neo-classical house was built for John, First Earl Spencer, the great-grandson of the great Duke of Marlborough. Completed in 1766 by John Stuart, it is considered one of the finest 18th-century London townhouses. The Spencer family lived in the house until the 1920s. Lord Rothschild purchased the lease on the property when the Spencer home was moved to Althorp, where Princess Diana is buried today. Today the Spencer house has been lovingly restored and is accessible by guided tours on Sundays.

Spencer House

Admission charge; Open to guided one-hour tours on Sundays (except during January and August) 10:30 a.m. - 5:45 p.m. (last admission 4:45 p.m.). Individual tickets must be purchased in person at the ticket desk at the entrance and cannot be booked in advance. Check its Web site, www.spencerhouse.co.uk.

Retrace your steps up Cleveland Row past the gatehouse towards Pall Mall, and then turn right onto the red pavement of Marlborough Road. Across Marlborough Road, you will see the temple-like façade of the Queen's Chapel. It was designed by Inigo Jones and built in 1627 as a Catholic chapel for Charles I's prospective bride, Infanta Maria of Spain. The Chapel was remodeled by Christopher Wren for Catherine of Braganza, Charles II's wife, after the Restoration of the Monarchy. St. James's Palace is closed to the public, but the Chapel Royal and Queen's Chapel are open to the public for worship services at certain times of the year.

Chapel Royal/ Queen's Chapel

The Chapel Royal is open to the public for Sunday worship services October - Good Friday from 8:30 a.m. - 11:30 a.m. The Queen's Chapel is open to the public for Sunday worship services Easter - October from 8:30 a.m. - 11:30 a.m.

Carefully cross over Marlborough Road. Walk past the entrance to the Queen's Chapel until you come to the beautiful Art Nouveau memorial dedicated to Queen Alexandra by Sir Alfred Gilbert—famous for Piccadilly's "Eros." Hear the tale of Queen Alexandra, the long-suffering wife of the philandering Edward VII, and discover the astonishing connection between Edward VII's longtime mistress, Mrs. Keppel, and today's Prince Charles. Step back to peer over the wall to see the top of Marlborough House. It was designed by Sir Christopher Wren in 1710 for the Duke of Marlborough.

Inigo Jones's Queen's Chapel.

Turn and stand for a moment with your back to the Alexandra memorial. The open area before you is the Friary Court. Listen as the narrator describes how the 18-year-old Queen Victoria made her first appearance to her subjects here on the balcony you see above the Court.

To reach the starting point for the eleventh tour, continue walking down Marlborough Road until you come to the Mall—the broad ceremonial boulevard which extends from the Admiralty Arch down on your left and leads to the gates of Buckingham Palace down on your right. After you cross over the Mall, enter St. James's Park through the elaborate iron gates, where the narration for the next tour begins. You will find public restrooms located to your right just inside the park.

Sir Alfred Gilbert's Art Nouveau-style
Queen Alexandra Memorial.

T O U R   1 1
(CD Two Track 11)

TOUR OF ST. JAMES'S PARK

"The happiness of London is not to be conceived,
but by those who have been in it. I will venture to say,
there is more learning and science within the
circumference of ten miles from where we now sit,
than in all the rest of the world."

James Boswell, *The Life of Samuel Johnson*

The eleventh tour, found on Track 11 of CD Two, begins just inside the gates into St. James's Park across from Marlborough Road. (See map page 56.) Follow the signs to the bridge over St. James's Lake, where you will enjoy some of London's most unforgettable views. The bridge

offers a spectacular view of Buckingham Palace and the Queen Victoria Monument across the lake. On the other side you will see the domed rooftops of Whitehall, and Horse Guards Parade, as well as the London Eye rising over the treetops in the distance. Listen as the narrator describes the development of this Royal Park, which began as a swampy marshland behind the leper colony of St. James. First, Henry VIII drained the swamp and enclosed the area as his private hunting preserve. Next, James I established his menagerie here. Finally, his grandson, Charles II, built aviaries along the south side of the park, leading to today's name, Birdcage Walk. The park still teems with swans, geese, ducks, and other exotic wildfowl, including pelicans, which are descended from a pair of pelicans that were presented to Charles II by the Russian ambassador.

St. James's Park

Admission free; Open daily dawn to dusk. Check out the Royal Parks' Web site, www.royalparks.com.

Continue on across the bridge and turn right. Follow the path along the water. When you approach the children's playground, you will bear left up the slight incline and exit St. James's Park onto Spur Road, which runs off

Birdcage Walk. Then turn right and go to the crosswalk to safely cross Spur Road. Turn right and go through the elaborate gates leading to the front of Buckingham Palace. Across from the center gates of the palace stands the gleaming white marble memorial to Queen Victoria, where the narration for the final tour begins.

(top) View towards Whitehall.
(above) View towards Buckingham Palace.

T O U R   1 2
(CD Two Track 12)

Tour of exterior of Buckingham Palace and the Queen Victoria Monument

"There is no doubt that of all the institutions,
which have grown up among us over the centuries or
sprung into being in our lifetime,
the Constitutional Monarchy is the most deeply
founded and dearly cherished."

Winston Churchill,
Prime Minister, 1940 -1945 and 1951-1955

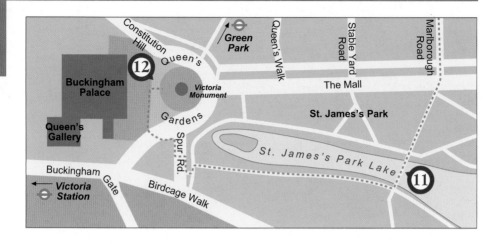

The twelfth and final tour of *Royal London In Context*, found on Track 12 of CD Two, begins on the steps of the memorial to Queen Victoria. Stand facing the gates of Buckingham Palace, the official London residence of Queen Elizabeth II, Britain's reigning monarch, and learn about the history of this proud symbol of the Royal Family. Depending on the unpredictable British weather, the world-renowned Changing of the Guard takes place here in the forecourt of Buckingham Palace daily, beginning at 11:30 a.m., from April until the end of July and then on alternate days for the rest of the year. There is no ceremony in wet weather. You will need to arrive early to pick out a good spot to view this very popular ceremony. (For more tips about attending the Changing of the Guard, see page 124.)

The Queen Victoria Monument stands in front of Buckingham Palace.

Listen as the narrator relates the colorful history behind the palace, which began as the townhouse of the Duke of Buckingham and went though long and tortuous renovations that outlasted the reigns of four monarchs before Queen Victoria finally made Buckingham Palace her London residence at her accession in 1837. You can see the central balcony on the sec-

Stately gates of Buckingham Palace.

ond floor where the Royal Family makes its formal public appearances to the crowds that throng around the Victoria Monument on important public occasions. Queen Elizabeth and her husband, Phillip, Duke of Edinburgh, live in a suite of 12 rooms on the second floor of the north wing over-looking Green Park.

Walk around to the front of the gleaming white memorial and observe the enormous figure of Queen Victoria, which sits facing up the Mall towards Admiralty Arch. Listen as you learn about the life of Queen Victoria—the longest-reigning monarch in British history. You may be sur-

The famed Changing of the Guard.

The monumental figure of Queen Victoria gazes down the Mall.

Crowds line up early to view the Changing of the Guard.

prised to discover that the beloved figure we remember from history was not always popular and survived many assassination attempts. Listen as the narrator relates the many trials and tribulations that Queen Victoria endured in her record 64-year reign until her death in 1901 at age 81.

Our final tour concludes here as we consider the many challenges facing Queen Elizabeth II, who is now the longest-reigning monarch after Queen Victoria, and we contemplate the future role of the British monarchy as it heads into the 21st century. You may wish to continue your exploration of Royal London by visiting the nearby Queen's Gallery and the Royal Mews, which are located on Buckingham Palace Road. (For more tips about visiting the Queen's Gallery and the Royal Mews, see pages 125-127.)

Buckingham Palace

Admission charge; Open mid August – September: 9:30 a.m. - 4:30 p.m. All tickets are by timed entry. (For more about the history of Buckingham Palace and ticketing information, see page 138.)

Canada Gate by Buckingham Palace and Green Park.

CHAPTER 2
A HISTORY OF THE BRITISH KINGS AND QUEENS

The British Isles have been inhabited since the last Ice Age. Beginning in the 8th century B.C., Celtic tribes began crossing the channel from mainland Europe and spreading out over the islands. In 55 and 54 B.C., Julius Caesar made brief forays into the southern part of the islands, but retreated after being battered by bad weather and fierce resistance from local inhabitants. The Romans returned with 40,000 soldiers in A.D. 43 to subjugate the local tribes and turn the islands into a colony, which they called *Britannia*. For nearly four centuries, Rome ruled Britain with an iron fist. The Romans built a bridge at a ford in the river Thames. A settlement grew up alongside the wooden bridge, which became the Roman city of *Londinium*, today's London.

During Nero's reign in A.D. 60, Queen Boudicca led her Iceni tribe in revolt against the brutality of Roman rule. *Londinium* was burned to the ground and its inhabitants were slaughtered. *Londinium* was rebuilt—this time with sturdy walls. The city prospered as a principal trade center and was made the Roman capital of *Britannia*. The Roman Legions were called home in A.D. 410 to defend Rome as its Empire began to crumble under the onslaught of waves of barbarian tribes. Britain was left to defend itself. The Dark Ages came as Picts and Scots swept down from the north. Irish tribes moved in from the west. Germanic tribes—the Jutes and Saxons, and Angles—crossed the channel to take control of the south, giving rise to the name England (from "Angles' Land").

The Saxon Kings, House of Wessex (802-1016)

Egbert was the first Saxon leader able to unite the many independent kingdoms and tribes under one rule. He is considered to be the first true King of England. Beginning in the 9th century A.D., the islands were again battered by a new series of destructive incursions from the Vikings (also called Norsemen or Danes). The Saxons, led by Egbert's grandson, King Alfred the Great, routed the Viking forces in 878. He is the only English king to be called "Great." Alfred retook London, restored its ancient Roman walls, and gave his kingdom decades of relative peace and prosperity. Alfred could both read and write and supported the translation of important Latin works into Anglo-Saxon. He established the first English seats of learning and introduced a legal code administered by the local reeves of the shires (source of the term "sheriffs").

The Danish Kings (1014-1042)

Alfred's successors were unsuccessful in appeasing the Vikings with annual tributes ("Danegeld"), and the Norsemen soon resumed their raids. In 1016, the Norse leader Canute defeated the Saxons led by Ethelred II. Canute established himself as ruler of Denmark, Norway, and England and made London his capital. The Saxon King Ethelred II, his wife Emma, and their son Edward fled into exile to Normandy in northern France. When Ethelred II died, his widow Emma married Canute, and Edward became Canute's stepson.

The Saxon Kings, House of Wessex Restored (1042-1066)

Canute's son and successor Hardicanute died in 1042. Anglo-Saxon rule of England was briefly restored when Edward succeeded his half-brother. Edward secured Saxon support by his marriage to Edith, the daughter of the powerful Saxon noble Earl Godwin of Wessex. Edward (known for his piety as Edward the Confessor) was far more interested in matters of religion than government and moved his court from the crowded confines of London to a new palace upriver, near the abbey church of St. Peter. The abbey was called Westminster ("West Monastery" in the Saxon dialect) to distinguish it from the monastery near St. Paul's Cathedral in the east.

For a time, the pious King seemed satisfied to let his wife's family run the country, but the Godwins opposed the favoritism shown by Edward to his Norman supporters. In 1051, Edward struck back. He locked his queen in a nunnery and tried to exile the Godwin family, but the Godwins returned with an army. A fragile peace was established when Edward restored Godwin and his sons to their titles and lands, but tensions between the Saxon and Norman factions at court continued to simmer.

Edward showed no inclination to produce an heir and favored as his successor his second cousin, William of Normandy (the illegitimate son of the Duke of Normandy and a tanner's daughter) called "William the Bastard." Although Edward's brother-in-law, Harold Godwinson, had sworn an oath to support William's claim to the throne, he reneged on his pledge when Edward the Confessor died in 1066. Harold claimed that the dying King had changed his mind and appointed him as his successor. Backed by the Saxon nobles eager to rid England of Norman influence, Harold II took the throne, but had little time to celebrate as the kingdom was immediately

Bayeux tapestry segment showing Harold pledging his loyalty to William.

threatened with invasion from the north by his brother, Tostig, who was supported by Harald Hardrada, King of Norway. Harold rushed north and defeated his traitorous brother in the Battle of Stamford Bridge.

In the meantime, William crossed the English Channel with an army of 50,000 men to claim the throne. Their forces clashed at Senlac Hill, just north of Hastings, in the pivotal Battle of Hastings. Even though Harold had hurried south to face the Norman advance, his Saxons almost won the day. William had three horses shot from under him in the ferocious fighting. According to legend, when an arrow pierced King Harold's eye, William's forces rushed forward to slaughter Harold and his brothers.

House of Normandy (1066-1154)

On Christmas Day 1066, William I was crowned as he stood in triumph over the tomb of Edward the Confessor. Westminster Abbey had been consecrated just the year before on December 28, 1065, but Edward had been too ill to attend. Edward died soon afterwards and was buried in his beloved abbey. "William the Conqueror" spent the remaining 21 years of his rule brutally crushing Saxon resistance and consolidating his power with ruthless efficiency, giving confiscated Saxon lands to his Norman supporters and building a string of fortified castles across England, including the great Tower of London. To more accurately tax his new subjects, he had an exhaustive survey made of the resources and wealth of his new kingdom. Completed in 1086, the comprehensive inventory was called the *Domesday Book*.

William died while fighting in Normandy. His horse stumbled on a burning cinder and the King was thrown forward. The horn of the saddle gouged his side, causing fatal internal injuries. He was succeeded by his third son, William II—nicknamed "William Rufus" for his red hair and flushed face. He made Westminster the administrative center of the kingdom and built Westminster Hall. His 12-year rule, marked by power struggles with the church, ended when the he was killed in a suspicious accident while out hunting with his younger brother Henry; an arrow shot by Walter Tirel hit the King squarely in the chest. Henry's elder brother Robert, who was next in line to the throne, was conveniently away on crusade. Henry left his dead brother's body in the forest and galloped off to seize the Royal Treasury. Tirel fled to France, but his son was allowed to keep his father's English estates, which led many to believe that William's "accident" was a well-timed assassination.

Henry I was crowned at Westminster Abbey in 1100. By the time his older brother returned, Henry was firmly in control. Henry—nicknamed *Beauclerc* ("good scholar") because, unlike his father, he could read and write—was a good administrator and ably ruled for 35 years until he died from food poisoning after gorging on a feast of lamprey eels.

With no surviving son, Henry appointed his nephew Stephen as ruler of his Norman territories in France, but named his daughter Matilda (also known as Maud) as heir to the English throne. Matilda had been wed as a young girl to the Holy Roman Emperor Henry V. After the death of her first husband, Matilda married the powerful Geoffrey Plantagenet, Count of Anjou. When Henry died, Matilda was with her husband in France. The King's nephew Stephen seized power and was crowned at Westminster Abbey on December 26, 1135, leading to a 19-year civil war. In the Treaty of Winchester it was agreed that Stephen would retain the throne, but the crown would pass to Matilda's son, Henry, at his death.

Plantagenets (House of Anjou) (1154-1399)

When Stephen died in 1154, Matilda's 21-year-old son by her second husband, Geoffrey, Count of Anjou, ascended to the throne as Henry II. Henry II, the great-grandson of William the Conqueror, was the first of thirteen kings of the Plantagenet dynasty who ruled England for the next 331 years. The family name of the Counts of Anjou came from the sprig of the flowering broom—*Planta genista*—that Henry's father wore as his battle emblem. Henry II was already master of much of France. A dynamic King, he is remembered today for his beautiful wife, Eleanor of Aquitaine, and his struggles with his unfaithful sons.

Henry battled to rein in his nobles and the clergy, who had grown powerful during the turmoil of Stephen's disputed reign. Henry appointed his good friend, Thomas Becket, as his Lord Chancellor and later made

Thomas Archbishop of Canterbury—even though the worldly Becket had never even been a priest. Thomas turned on Henry and became devoted to protecting the rights of the church. Thomas vigorously opposed the King's efforts to bring the clergy under the crown's control and have clergymen who were charged with serious crimes tried in royal courts.

Legend says that Henry exclaimed, "Will no one rid me of this troublesome priest?" before four of Henry's knights rode off to Canterbury and murdered Thomas on December 29, 1170, while he was saying Mass. The sacrilege so outraged the people that Henry was flogged by monks as penance at his old friend's tomb at Canterbury. Thomas was made a saint only three years later by Pope Alexander. In 1220, Becket's remains were entombed in a shrine behind the high altar in Canterbury, which became a popular place of pilgrimage.

Despite his struggles with the church, Henry was a strong administrator who introduced important legal reforms, such as a jury of twelve men (replacing trial by combat). Henry's final years were spent battling with his wife, Eleanor, and his rebellious sons as they each jockeyed for position as his successor. Henry died at age 56 in France. When Richard (Henry's third son and eventual successor) came to view his dead father's body, legend says the corpse suddenly began to bleed from the nose.

Richard I was crowned at Westminster Abbey in 1189. Known as Richard *Coeur-de-Lion* ("Lion-Heart"), this colorful warrior-king of England spent little more than six months in England during his entire 10-year reign. His wife, Queen Berengaria of Navarre, never even set foot there. Raised in Poitiers, France, by his mother, Eleanor, Richard cared little for his new kingdom and spent most of his reign unsuccessfully trying to reclaim the Holy Land from Saladin's army in the Third Crusade. Returning from the Holy Land, Richard was captured by the Holy Roman Emperor Henry VI and held for over a year, while his brother, John, nearly bankrupted England taxing his subjects to raise the King's ransom. Richard returned to England only briefly before returning to France, where he died at age 41.

Richard's death left John to rule over a land weary from taxation. Nicknamed "Lackland" because Henry II had left his youngest son no territories, John was inept as a soldier and soon lost the hard-won French territories conquered by Richard and Henry. When John clashed with Pope Innocent III, the Pope excommunicated the King, issued an Interdict banning all church services in England except baptisms and burials, and later declared that John was no longer the rightful king. In 1215, rebellious English nobles confronted the King in a meadow at Runnymede not far from Windsor Castle, where he was forced to sign the *Magna Carta* (Latin for the "Great Charter") guaranteeing the barons' rights and limiting the king's power. As soon as he was free from his nobles, John reneged on his word. Hostilities resumed and continued until his death in 1216.

John's 9-year-old son succeeded him as Henry III, with regents ruling on his behalf. Henry III tried to take over the reins of government in 1227, but nobles led by the King's brother-in-law, Simon de Montfort, rose up in rebellion. The "Great Council"—the forerunner of Parliament—was called to discuss the barons' grievances. Henry was forced to sign the Provisions of Oxford limiting his power, but the uneasy coalition splintered into factions. The King's son, Prince Edward, killed de Montfort in the Battle of Evesham. Henry III died in 1272 at the age of 65, after a 56-year reign. Henry III's finest legacy was rebuilding Westminster Abbey as a grand shrine to honor his ancestor, King Edward the Confessor, who had been made a saint in 1161.

The weak-willed Henry III was succeeded by his eldest son, Edward I, who became one of England's most successful rulers. Nicknamed "Edward Longshanks" for his 6-foot height, Edward was a capable soldier. He was also called the "Hammer of the Scots" for his victories over the Scots in his attempts to unite England and Scotland. He brought the Scottish coronation stone—the fabled "Stone of Scone"—back to Westminster Palace, where it remained under the monarch's coronation throne until it was returned to Scotland in 1996.

At age 15, Edward was married to the 13-year-old Eleanor, Infanta of Castile. At first a political match, they grew to be devoted to one another. Eleanor bore Edward 16 children. She died while traveling north to meet the King. The grief-stricken King erected a memorial cross at each spot where the funeral procession rested for the night as it made its way back to Westminster Abbey for the Queen's burial. The last stop was near the small village of Charing. A large cross was erected there at the southern end of today's Trafalgar Square. It was torn down by Cromwell's men during the Civil War.

Edward I conquered Wales and pledged his firstborn son as their prince—the first Prince of Wales—and it became customary for the heir to the throne to receive that title. The Scots rose again under William Wallace (of *Braveheart* fame) and defeated Edward's army in the Battle of Stirling

Bridge, only to be beaten two years later at the Battle of Falkirk. Wallace escaped, but later was betrayed and turned over to the English. Wallace was hanged, drawn and quartered, and his head was stuck on a pole atop London Bridge.

Jews had held on precariously in England as the kingdom's principal moneylenders. In 1290, Edward expelled all Jews from England on charges of usury. The Lombards and Venetians of Northern Italy hurried to London to replace Jewish bankers, settling around Lombard Street, which remains the financial heart of modern London. In 1295, Edward summoned his nobles, churchmen, and representatives from the shires and towns to the so-called "Model Parliament," where the King worked to codify English law and standardize the collection of taxes.

Edward died at 68, while once again on the march against the Scots. He was succeeded by his son Edward II, who is generally acknowledged to be one of England's worst monarchs. As a young man, Edward became enamored of a handsome young knight from Gascony, Piers Gaveston. Edward's father had exiled Gaveston, but when the old King died, Gaveston returned to London where he smugly carried the King's crown in the coronation. Edward showered gifts and honors on his favorite and made Gaveston Earl of Cornwall. Gaveston was later kidnapped and murdered by the King's enemies. In 1314, Edward personally led his army into a disastrous campaign against the Scottish King, Robert the Bruce, narrowly escaping with his life when the English army was routed at the Battle of Bannockburn.

Despite his predilection for handsome young men, Edward II married Isabella (sister of France's King Charles IV) who bore him four children before she abandoned him for her lover, Roger Mortimer. Isabella tried to seize power in the name of their son. She forced Edward to abdicate, and imprisoned him in Berkeley Castle. To make the King's death appear natural, his killers inserted a red-hot poker into his bowels through a hollowed horn, leaving no marks on the King's body. His 14-year-old son was crowned Edward III, but Isabella lost her bid for power when the Parliament set up a Regency Council to govern on the young King's behalf. Three years after his father's murder, Edward took control of the government, imprisoned his mother, and had her lover, Roger Mortimer, executed.

Edward III worked to restore good relations with his barons before igniting the "Hundred Years War" by claiming the throne of France when his uncle, France's Charles IV, died without an heir. Edward III led the English army to victory in the Battle of Crécy. His eldest son was known as the "Black Prince" for the black armor he wore in battle. He defeated the French in the Battle of Poitiers in 1356.

Fascinated with the legend of King Arthur and the ideals of Christian chivalry, Edward III founded the Order of Knights of the Garter in 1348. Under Edward's reign, Parliament grew in power and was divided into two houses—one for the nobility and the other for commoners, which has evolved into the House of Lords and House of Commons.

The successes of Edward's reign were overshadowed by the bubonic plague, which had spread from Europe in 1348. Nearly one-third of the kingdom's population died within ten years, devastating the economy. The King's last days were saddened by the death in 1376 of his much-loved son and heir, Edward, the Black Prince. The following year, Edward III died of a stroke at age 64 and was succeeded by his 10-year-old grandson Richard II.

Richard II had no formal regent, but his uncles, John of Gaunt, Duke of Lancaster, and Thomas, Duke of Gloucester, stepped into the vacuum. They were ousted by a coalition of nobles, known as the "Lords Appellant," who governed the country. The young King showed his father's courage by bravely riding out to quiet an unruly mob during the Peasant's Revolt in 1381 (Wat Tyler's Rebellion). The people had risen up against a poll tax imposed to pay for the long years of war against France. In 1389, Richard seized control and arrested the Lords Appellant, executing some and banishing others. Richard II alienated his nobles by trying to reassert royal authority. In 1399, while Richard was away putting down a rebellion in Ireland, his exiled cousin, Henry of Bolingbroke, landed in Yorkshire with a small army. The disgruntled barons sided with Henry, Richard was deposed, and, with the blessing of Parliament, Henry usurped the throne as Henry IV. Richard died in prison the following year, probably from starvation.

Plantagenets (House of Lancaster) (1399-1471)

King Henry IV's miserable 14-year reign was rocked by revolts, a recurrence of the plague, financial problems, and widespread popular unrest. Henry lived in constant fear of assassination, and in his last years suffered from a leprosy-like skin condition. A prophecy had said that Henry would die in Jerusalem, and so he prudently avoided the Holy Land. However, in 1413, when the King became sick while visiting Westminster

Abbey, he was taken to a meeting room called the "Jerusalem Chamber." When he realized where he had been taken, Henry cried out in anguish that the prophecy had been fulfilled. He died hours later at age 55.

Henry was succeeded by his energetic and capable son, Henry V. Even though he ruled for only nine years, Henry V is remembered as one of the great warrior-kings of England. He gathered the support of his barons and then crossed the English Channel to assert his claim to the throne of France. In the famous Battle of Agincourt in 1415, Henry's forces were outnumbered three to one, but (as celebrated in Shakespeare's play *Henry V*) the longbows of the English and Welsh archers mowed down the ranks of the French knights in a ghastly slaughter. It was said the French lost 6,000 men, while English losses numbered fewer than 400. Henry V forced France's King Charles VI to accept him as the future heir to the French throne, sealing the pact by taking Charles' daughter, Catherine of Valois, as his bride.

Henry V's gains were short-lived. He died of dysentery two years later at the age of 35, before he could succeed to the French throne, leaving an 8-month-old son as heir. During Henry VI's minority, power was shared between his uncles, John, Duke of Bedford, as Regent of France and Humphrey, Duke of Gloucester, as Regent of England. The unfortunate Henry VI became a pawn in the disastrous 85-year-long war as the two branches of the Plantagenet Royal Family—the House of Lancaster and the House of York—battled for power. It came to be known as the "Wars of the Roses" from the white and red roses which were the emblems of the two rival houses.

Bedford's attempt to conquer France was stalled in the siege of Orléans. In 1429, a 17-year-old peasant girl called Joan of Arc appeared from the countryside and energized the French to expel the English invaders. The French-backed heir was crowned King Charles VII at Rheims. In 1431, Joan of Arc was burned at the stake in Rouen, condemned as a witch and a heretic by the English. But by 1453, the English had been driven out of France except for the port city of Calais, which England held until 1558.

Henry VI tried to assume rule in 1437, but was too ineffectual to prevent infighting among his nobles and suffered a mental breakdown in 1454. Civil war broke out between the followers of Richard, Duke of York (a descendant of Edward III), who sought to depose Henry as unfit to rule, and the supporters of Henry and the Lancaster family. Richard was killed in 1460 during the Battle of Wakefield, but Richard's son Edward took up his father's campaign. He deposed Henry VI in 1461 and was crowned as King Edward IV. Henry was thrown into the Tower of London.

Plantagenets (House of York) (1461-1485)

Edward IV's ascension to the throne was rubber-stamped by Parliament. From 1461 until 1470, the country enjoyed nine brief years of relative peace, before Edward IV was driven into exile by a coalition led by Henry's wife, Margaret of Anjou. Edward returned to power in 1471 and Henry VI was murdered in the Tower of London. The last twelve years of Edward IV's reign saw increased trade and prosperity.

The nation's troubles resumed after Edward IV's death, when the throne passed to his 13-year-old son, Edward V. Appointed as Protector, the young King's uncle, Richard, Duke of Gloucester, took Edward V and his young brother, Richard, to the supposed "safety" of the Tower of London. The "Little Princes" were never seen again. Coerced by Richard, Parliament declared his two nephews illegitimate and crowned him Richard III. His 5-year reign ended in 1485 when he was killed by Henry Tudor in the Battle of Bosworth Field. According to a popular tale, Richard's crown fell from his head during the battle and landed on a hawthorn bush. It was retrieved by Lord Stanley, who placed it on Henry Tudor's head, ushering in the rule of the House of Tudor.

House of Tudor (1485-1603)

Henry was the great-great-great-grandson of Edward II and had only a tenuous claim to the throne. However, his marriage to Elizabeth of York (eldest daughter of Edward IV and sister to the Little Princes who perished in the Tower) united the Houses of York and Lancaster and brought an end to their ruinous, long-running conflict. Pope Innocent VIII formally recognized Henry's right to the throne in 1486, and peace returned to England.

Henry VII ruled ably for 24 years. He avoided foreign adventures. His frugal, prudent policies at home brought stability and security. To cement an alliance with Spain, the King's heir apparent, the 14-year-old Prince Arthur, was married by proxy to the Spanish princess, Catherine of Aragon, daughter of Ferdinand of Aragon and Isabella of Castile (who financed the voyage of Columbus to the New World). Henry's daughter Margaret was wed to James IV, King of Scotland, paving the way for the Scottish King James VI to eventually succeed Henry VII's granddaughter, Elizabeth I, in 1603.

Henry VII's later years were filled with private sadness. His adored son and heir, Prince Arthur, died unexpectedly in 1503 and Henry's wife died in childbirth ten months later. Henry VII died in 1509 and was buried beside his wife in their tomb in the Lady Chapel at Westminster Abbey.

The King's second son, Henry, was not quite 18 when he ascended to the throne as Henry VIII. He had been well-schooled and could read and write Latin and French. He was a superb athlete, horseman, hunter, dancer, musician, poet, and soldier, but he was also a ruthless and mercurial ruler who executed an estimated 72,000 people during his 38-year reign.

Han Holbein's portrait of Henry VIII.

His father left him a peaceful, unified country and a bountiful treasury. Henry married his brother's widow, Catherine, and tried to force his way onto the European political stage by joining his father-in-law (Ferdinand of Aragon), Pope Julius II, and the Republic of Venice in the "Holy League" against France. Henry personally led his troops in a few minor battles in France before peace was negotiated by Thomas Wolsey, who had quickly risen through the ranks of the church before he was made Henry's Lord Chancellor in 1515. In 1520, Wolsey arranged a peace summit between Henry and France's King Francis I called "the Field of the Cloth of Gold" for the ostentatious display, lavish feasts, and extravagant tournaments held as each young king tried to outshine the other.

After Martin Luther posted his 95 Theses in 1517, protesting against the abuses of the Roman Catholic Church, Henry wrote *Defense of the Seven Sacraments* in rebuttal (no doubt with the help of his friend, Thomas More, and his former teacher, John Fisher), which was widely read across Europe. For his support of the Catholic faith, the Pope bestowed on Henry the title of "Defender of the Faith"—a title carried by each English monarch to this day.

Henry's wife, Catherine, gave birth to six children, but only their daughter Mary survived. When Catherine failed to bear a son after nearly 20 years of marriage, Henry became convinced that God was punishing him for marrying his brother's widow. By the time Catherine had turned 40, Henry despaired that she would never give him the legitimate son and heir he felt was needed to carry on the House of Tudor. The King sought to divorce Catherine, but she contested the divorce and challenged Henry to deny that she had been a virgin at their marriage. While desperately seeking a way out of his marriage, the King became infatuated with the young Anne Boleyn.

The King commanded that Wolsey obtain Pope Clement VII's permission for his divorce. This posed an insurmountable dilemma for the Pope, as Catherine's nephew was Charles V, the Holy Roman Emperor and King of Spain, whose forces had recently sacked Rome and had held the Pope a prisoner. Charles pressured Clement not to grant the divorce. Wolsey went to Italy to personally plead the King's case with the Pope, but he failed. The King charged Wolsey with treason and confiscated Wolsey's grand homes at Hampton Court and York House. Only Wolsey's sudden death on the way to meet the King saved him from prison and the chopping block.

Thomas Cromwell, Henry's new chief advisor, encouraged the King to break from the Roman Catholic Church and establish himself as the head of a new Church of England. Henry's newly appointed Archbishop of Canterbury, Thomas Cranmer, granted the King's divorce on his own authority in 1533. Henry then hurriedly married Anne Boleyn, who gave birth to Princess Elizabeth some eight months later. The Pope refused to recognize the divorce and declared the marriage void.

Henry's lifelong friend Sir Thomas More became Lord Chancellor after Wolsey's fall from grace. A devout Catholic, More resigned when he saw Henry's coming break with Rome. After the Pope excommunicated Henry in 1533, the Act of Supremacy was passed declaring Henry as the head of the new Church of England. More was beheaded for refusing to take an oath recognizing Henry as the Supreme Head of the Church.

When Anne gave birth to a girl, Princess Elizabeth, Henry was so furious he refused to attend the infant's christening. Elizabeth was followed by two stillborn children and a miscarriage. Henry grew tired of Anne and cast about for some excuse to get rid of her. She was arrested on trumped-up charges of treason and witchcraft in beguiling the King. As proof, her accus-ers pointed out Anne bore the sign of the devil—six fingers on her left hand—a matter overlooked by Henry during his lusty courtship. Anne was accused of adultery and even incest with her brother George. Archbishop Cranmer again succumbed to the King's will and declared Anne's marriage to Henry null. Two days later, Anne was beheaded on Tower Green. Henry, who was enjoying a game of tennis when he heard the cannon fire from the Tower of London announcing Anne's execution, hurried off to the house of Jane Seymour, one of Anne's Ladies-in-Waiting, who had caught the King's eye. He married her eleven days later.

Under Thomas Cromwell's urging, Henry began the dissolution of the monasteries. The King started by seizing the properties of the smaller monasteries and convents. Confiscated lands were then sold to Henry's supporters. The remaining church properties were seized in 1539. Even Westminster Abbey ceased to be a monastery church in 1540 and was stripped of its art and relics.

Jane Seymour died in 1537, twelve days after giving birth to the future Edward VI. Thomas Cromwell proposed the Flemish Anne of Cleves as a new bride to strengthen England's ties with the Low Countries. Relying on a flattering portrait by Hans Holbein, Henry accepted a proxy marriage, but when Henry met his new bride at Greenwich Palace, he was appalled, call-ing her "The Mare of Flanders." The marriage was never consummated, and he promptly divorced her.

Henry's roving eye was caught by a 19-year-old named Catherine Howard, Anne Boleyn's first cousin. The King became infatuated with the striking beauty who was 30 years his junior, calling Catherine "a rose with-out a thorn." They were married three weeks after his divorce from Anne of Cleves. Henry was unaware that Catherine had enjoyed the favors of many lovers before her marriage to the King. Soon after their wedding, there were rumors that Catherine had resumed her affairs behind the King's back. When the King learned of Catherine's infidelity, Catherine was arrest-ed for treason and was beheaded after just seventeen months of marriage.

The following year the indefatigable Henry married the 30-year-old, twice-widowed Catherine Parr, even though at the time she was engaged to wed Thomas Seymour, the brother of Jane Seymour, Henry's third wife. Catherine Parr was a solid, comfortable spouse. She took good care of the aging and dissipated King and looked after his young heir, Edward, and his daughters, Mary and Elizabeth, until Henry's death at age 55. After the King's death, Catherine married her original intended, Thomas Seymour.

Henry VIII died in 1547, believing he had ensured the succession of the house of Tudor with his long-desired male heir. Henry's 9-year-old son, Edward VI, came to the throne surrounded on all sides by competing factions. His uncle, Edward Seymour, Earl of Hertford, became Duke of Somerset and Protector of the Realm, but was ousted three years later by John Dudley, Duke of Northumberland.

Edward was a sickly child, possibly suffering from tuberculosis or congenital syphilis contracted from his father. Henry VIII's will had provided that his eldest daughter, Mary, would succeed to the throne if Edward died without children. When Edward VI died after reigning for only six years, Lady Jane Grey was declared Queen through the intrigue of her father-in-law, the Duke of Northumberland, who persuaded the dying Edward that the 16-year-old Protestant Lady Jane (whose grandmother was Henry VIII's younger sister) was far preferable to Edward's rabidly Catholic half-sister, Mary. Lady Jane's reign lasted a mere nine days before Mary seized control. Northumberland and Lady Jane were beheaded.

Mary, the daughter of Henry VIII and his first wife, Catherine of Aragon, had been declared a bastard, when her father divorced her mother. Mary was even forced to serve as a maid to her baby sister, Elizabeth, until Elizabeth's mother was beheaded. Mary resolved to bring England back into the Roman Catholic fold by force. Known as "Bloody Mary," she sent over 300 Protestants to be burned at the stake, including Bishops Ridley and Latimer and Henry VIII's Archbishop of Canterbury, the ever-pliant Thomas Cranmer. Cardinal Reginald Pole (whose 70-year-old mother, Margaret Pole, Countess of Salisbury, had been executed by Henry VIII in 1541) returned to England to assist in Mary's efforts and was made Mary's new Archbishop of Canterbury.

In 1554, Mary married Philip II—the very Catholic King of Spain—who loathed Mary and stayed in Spain for most of Mary's reign. Despite two false pregnancies, Mary was never able to conceive the child who would ensure a Catholic heir to the throne. Philip persuaded Mary that England should join him in a war against France, but the campaign ended in disaster with England losing Calais—its last European possession. On her deathbed, she grudgingly recognized her half-sister Elizabeth as her successor.

Elizabeth, the daughter of Anne Boleyn, Henry VIII's second wife, became an outcast after her mother was beheaded. When Mary took the throne, Elizabeth was thrown into the Tower of London on charges of treason, barely escaping her mother's fate by pleading that she had no knowledge of any Protestant conspiracy against Mary. As there was no proof of her complicity, Elizabeth was eventually released.

Elizabeth came to the throne at the age of 25 and began a 45-year rule that established England as a preeminent world power. Intelligent and well-educated, she was reputed

Queen Elizabeth I.

to speak nine languages. The "Elizabethan Age," as it came to be called, witnessed the flowering of the English Renaissance with writers such as Christopher Marlowe, Ben Jonson, and playwright William Shakespeare, and explorers such as Sir Walter Raleigh, who founded a colony in America, which he named "Virginia" in honor of the "Virgin Queen."

When Pope Paul IV declared Elizabeth illegitimate with no right to the throne, the Queen restored her father's Church of England with herself at its head. She sought to keep her country out of war, while fending off repeated Catholic plots. Driven out of Scotland, her cousin, Mary, Queen of Scots, sought sanctuary in the north of England, where she became a focal point for pro-Catholic conspiracies. When a scheme to murder Elizabeth and place Mary on the throne was uncovered and it was shown that Mary was aware of the plot, Elizabeth reluctantly ordered her cousin's execution.

With Elizabeth's tacit approval, English privateers harassed and plundered Spanish ships bringing gold home from the New World. Elizabeth further antagonized the Spanish King, Philip II, by spurning his offers of marriage. When Mary, Queen of Scots, was executed, Philip pledged to bring down the heretic Queen. With the Pope's blessing, Philip mounted the famous Spanish Armada in 1588 to overthrow Elizabeth and restore the

Catholic faith in England.

The English navy destroyed many of Philip's ships in a preemptive nighttime attack against the Spanish Armada assembling at Cadiz, Spain. The surviving Spanish naval force continued on, but was hammered by storms off the coast of Britain. Philip launched a second Armada in 1596, and a third in 1597, but they, too, were pushed back by stormy seas. Spain's "invincible" Armada was defeated as much by the notoriously bad English weather as the skill of Elizabeth's naval commanders. Nevertheless, Elizabeth's victories confirmed England's status as the world's foremost naval power.

Elizabeth skillfully played one European power off the other as she dangled, and then withdrew, the prospects of a royal marriage. Ambitious courtiers used Elizabeth's vanity to rise at court. Her first love, the handsome Lord Robert Dudley, was with the Queen at Windsor Castle when his wife, Amy Robsart, died in a fall down a flight of stairs. The death was called accidental, but widespread suspicions over the convenient death ended Dudley's suitability as a royal consort.

While in her fifties, the spinster Queen became infatuated with the dashing young Robert Devereux, Earl of Essex, who was in his twenties. He was the stepson of her first lover, Robert Dudley. The youthful Essex played on the Queen's vanity and wrote love letters professing his undying affection. He extravagantly praised her beauty, even though Elizabeth was nearly bald, her face scarred from smallpox, and her teeth blackened from her indulgence in sugary treats. They quarreled and reconciled like adolescent lovers. The Queen named Essex to various military posts, but each mission ended in dismal failure. After a series of military misadventures, Essex was thrown into prison. Elizabeth relented and he was released, but the Queen's forgiving nature to her darling Essex did not extend to treason. In 1601, Essex foolishly misjudged the people's affection for their Queen and tried to overthrow her. He was arrested and summarily executed.

As early as 1586, Queen Elizabeth informally acknowledged her cousin James VI, King of Scotland, as her successor. He was the son of Mary, Queen of Scots, and the great-grandson of Margaret Tudor, the sister of Henry VIII and Elizabeth's aunt. James had been raised a Protestant, and his succession would ensure that Elizabeth's beloved country would not fall back under Catholicism. Two years before her death, Elizabeth spoke of her abiding affection for her subjects in a speech to the House of Commons affirming, "There is no prince that loves his subjects better, or whose love can countervail our love…. There is no jewel, be it never so rich a price, which I set before this jewel: I mean your love."

House of Stuart (1603-1649)

The Tudor dynasty ended with Queen Elizabeth I's death in 1603. The Queen's Privy Council confirmed her cousin James as her successor. James VI of Scotland took the throne of England as James I. His accession united the crowns of England and Scotland and marked the beginning of the Stuart dynasty. James fervently believed in the Divine Right of Kings and the idea that the king was God's anointed agent on earth. He also had enjoyed absolute authority in Scotland for 36 years. This set the crown on an inevitable collision course with the independent-minded English Parliament.

France's King Henry IV called James "the wisest fool in Christendom." The English did not know what to make of their new Scottish king. He was short, ungainly, coarse, and chronically ill, with legs so weak he often had to be supported when he walked. James also had an abnormally swollen tongue, which caused him to drool when he spoke. He constantly wore gloves and it was said that he never washed his hands. But James was a great patron of the arts. Flemish artists Rubens and Van Dyck were brought to London to glorify his reign with their paintings. James employed the architect Inigo Jones, who revolutionized English architecture with the introduction of the classical Italian style of Andrea Palladio called "Palladian." James I had grandiose plans for the reconstruction of the ramshackle palace of Whitehall to make it into an English Versailles, but he finished construction of only the Banqueting House before his death.

Early in his reign, pro-Catholic forces tried to assassinate the King by blowing up the House of Lords when James came to speak at the State Opening of Parliament. The Gunpowder Plot was foiled on November 5, 1606, when Guy Fawkes was discovered in the basement of Parliament with 30 barrels of gunpowder. Fawkes was taken to the Tower of London, where he was tortured until he confessed. Fawkes was put to death at Old Palace Yard at Westminster Palace. Guy Fawkes Day is still celebrated by the British each November 5th with bonfires and fireworks.

James was a man of contradictions. He locked Queen Elizabeth's former favorite, Sir Walter Raleigh, in the Tower of London for thirteen years, and yet he allowed Raleigh to tutor the King's children before he ordered

Raleigh to be beheaded in the Old Palace Yard. The King's eldest son, Henry, remarked that no one but his father would "keep such a bird in a cage." James was lukewarm in his support of Protestantism, and yet he sponsored the revised translation of the Bible that came to be known as the King James's Authorized Version—one of the most influential works in the English language. Although James had married Anne of Denmark and dutifully produced nine children, he was also notorious for his flagrant affairs with young men. After a parade of early favorites, the dashing George Villiers captured the King's life-long affections. Villiers' meteoric rise from Earl to Duke of Buckingham caused consternation at Court and friction with the conservative Parliament, but the King was unapologetic and declared, "You may be sure that I love the Earl of Buckingham more than anyone else . . . Christ had his John, I have my George." Such unorthodox sentiments did not sit well with the growing religious conservative movement in the Parliament. During James's reign a fundamentalist Protestant group called the Puritans began to gain control of Parliament. The Puritans sought to "purify" the church by ridding it of Catholic rituals. In 1620, a splinter group called the "Pilgrim Fathers" set sail for New England on the *Mayflower.*

The King's inept foreign policy and continual struggles with Parliament over money to sustain his extravagant lifestyle set the stage for the Civil War that erupted in his son's reign. James died in 1625 at age 58

Bust of Charles I outside St. Margaret's Church.

and was succeeded by his son, Charles I, who like his father, held an unshakeable belief in the Divine Right of Kings. The shy and stammering new King aligned himself with the strong-willed and unpopular George Villiers, Duke of Buckingham, his father's longtime favorite.

A year into Charles I's reign, Parliament accused Buckingham of wrongdoing. The King rejected their attempt to impeach his most-trusted advisor. In 1628, Parliament sought to restrain the King's actions with its Petition of Right. In retaliation, Charles dismissed Parliament and tried to rule without it for eleven years, borrowing heavily from his nobles and unilaterally imposing custom duties to raise revenues. Buckingham was killed by assassin John Felton in 1628. Felton had hoped to free the King from Buckingham's pro-Catholic grip, but Charles's wife, the French Catholic Henrietta Maria, quickly grew to exercise great influence over the King.

The strongly Presbyterian Scots rose up against the King's ill-advised attempt to impose the use of the Anglican prayer book. The King recalled Parliament in 1640 to raise money to put down the revolt, but the "Short Parliament" was dismissed within three weeks, after refusing to grant any money unless the King considered their grievances. The King refused to entertain any complaints against his God-ordained rule. Charles marched north, but failed to defeat the Scots. Now strapped for funds, the King summoned Parliament again. The leaders agreed to convene to consider raising funds only if Parliament could not be dissolved without its consent. One of the first acts of the "Long Parliament" was to pass the Grand Remonstrance, listing 201 objections to Charles's actions as monarch.

The outraged King personally forced his way into the House of Commons with armed guards. The King tried to arrest five of the ringleaders, but they had already fled. The English Civil War had begun, pitting the Royalists (called "Cavaliers") against the Puritan-dominated Parliamentarians (called "Roundheads" for their short-cropped hair).

Charles abandoned London and fled to the pro-Royalist city of Oxford, while his wife and younger children fled to France. The Parliamentarians raised an army based in London. The Royalists' early victory at the Battle of Edgehill was followed by successive defeats at Marston Moor and Naseby. The Parliamentarian forces held the upper hand with more money and men, and the brilliant military leadership of Thomas Fairfax and the young Oliver Cromwell. After four grinding years of war, the King surrendered to the Scottish army, which handed him over to Parliament.

The Commonwealth (1649-1659)

Charles was detained at Hampton Court, but he escaped and took refuge on the Isle of Wight, and tried to persuade the Scots to support an invasion of England. In the spring of 1648, the second phase of the Civil War began, but the Royalists were soon crushed by the Parliamentary forces led by Oliver Cromwell. The King was again imprisoned. Urged on by Cromwell, Charles was tried for treason. Charles defiantly refused to recognize their authority to try their king. By a mere one-vote margin—68 to 67— Charles was condemned to die. On January 30, 1649, Charles stepped out of the second story window of the Banqueting House on Whitehall Street onto scaffolding, where he was beheaded. A young witness wrote that the execution was met with "such a groan as I have never heard before and desire I may never hear again."

England was declared a Commonwealth with Oliver Cromwell as its Lord Protector. Cromwell abolished the

Lord Protector Oliver Cromwell.

House of Lords and ruled as absolute dictator, backed by his well-trained army—a king in all but name, although he nominally shared power with a Council of State and the unicameral Parliament. Faced with unrelenting quarrels between political factions, Cromwell dissolved his own Parliament.

Cromwell brutally suppressed a Royalist rebellion in Ireland and granted vast tracts of Ireland confiscated from the rebels to his Puritan supporters. When sporadic uprisings continued, Cromwell divided the country into districts and placed them under the direct administration of the military, which enforced the rigidly Puritanical laws enacted by Parliament. London found itself in the iron grip of the Puritan's zealous laws, which closed down all theatres, made drinking, gambling, and swearing criminal offenses, enforced the observance of the Sabbath, and even banned the celebration of Christmas, which was considered a Papist superstition. To Cromwell's credit, Jews were allowed back into England for the first time since the reign of Edward I.

Cromwell refused to accept the title of king, but he designated his son Richard to be his successor as Lord Protector. Cromwell died peacefully in his bed in 1658. After his father's death, Cromwell's son, nicknamed "Tumbledown Dick," could not control the army or manage the bickering political factions. He simply resigned, plunging the country into turmoil. In the chaos that followed, General George Monk, commander of the army occupying Scotland, marched south on London with his army. He recalled Parliament and sought to bring about the Restoration of the Monarchy, if the king would abide by certain conditions. In the Declaration of Breda, the eldest son of the executed Charles I promised a general amnesty to the anti-Royalists, guaranteed religious toleration, and agreed to pay the arrears in salary to the army.

Restoration of the House of Stuart (1660-1688)

Charles II entered London on May 30, 1660, his 30th birthday, and was joyously welcomed back by the people who were weary of Puritanical restrictions and exhausted by years of political uncertainty and military rule. The nine surviving Parliamentary leaders in the trial and execution of Charles I were arrested and put to death. On the anniversary of Charles I's execution, Cromwell's body was exhumed from Westminster Abbey, his corpse was ceremoniously hanged, drawn and quartered, and his severed head was placed atop a spire of Westminster Hall, where it remained for nearly a quarter century.

The House of Lords and House of Commons were restored. Charles ruled as king, but now it was clear that he acted by the grace of Parliament and had no power to impose taxes or arrest Members of Parliament. In a wave of Royalist sentiment, a largely pro-monarchist Parliament was elected in 1661, which sought to restore the Church of England and increase the king's authority.

"I will not venture a war nor travel again for any party," declared Charles. Known as the "Merry Monarch," Charles was determined to enjoy his reign. The pleasure-seeking King loved racing, gambling, and enjoying his beautiful mistresses, whom he showered with favors and titles. Louise de Kérouaille, who was created Duchess of Portsmouth, gave the King a son who was made Duke of Richmond. Barbara Villiers, who was mother to six of the King's illegitimate children, was made Duchess of Cleveland. The King's most famous mistress was Nell Gwynne, who as a young child once sold oranges to the patrons of the Drury Lane Theatre as she dreamed of appearing on stage. Nell became the lover of actor Charles Hart (William Shakespeare's grandnephew). In 1665, she made her debut in John Dryden's *Indian Queen*. Charles II saw her perform on stage and became captivated by her charms. Nell quickly became one of the King's favorite mistresses. She bore him several children; one was made the Duke of Albany. Nell was given a fine home in Pall Mall where she could be suitably close to the King's residence at St. James's Palace. When Charles II died in February, 1685, Nell was deeply in debt. The King made a deathbed plea to his brother James, "Let not poor Nelly starve." James settled her debts and looked after Nell until she suffered a stroke and died two years later. The longtime mistress to the King was buried in the Church of St. Martin-in-the-Fields.

Theater and dancing, long banned under Puritan rule, flourished under the Merry Monarch. The Theatre Royal Drury Lane in Covent Garden was granted its Royal Warrant in 1665. Charles was also a great patron of the arts and science. He built the Royal Observatory at Greenwich Palace. Charles's 15-year reign was buoyed by prosperity and a cultural renaissance with writers John Milton and John Bunyan, poets John Dryden and Samuel Butler, and diarists Samuel Pepys and John Evelyn. The King employed foreign artists including painter Peter Lely and wood carver Grinling Gibbons. Overseas trade was expanded. New colonies were established in New Jersey, Pennsylvania, Carolina, and Canada. New Amsterdam was captured from the Dutch in 1664 and renamed New York. The East India Company expanded its commercial influence in India.

After five heady years of the Restoration, Charles II's reign was marred by a series of natural disasters. The plague returned with a vengeance in 1665, killing more than 100,000 Londoners. The following year, just as the plague began to diminish, the city was ravaged by the Great Fire of London. On the night of September 2, 1666, a small fire started in a baker's shop in Pudding Lane, and the flames spread to destroy four-fifths of London in a conflagration that lasted four days. The commercial center of London was completely destroyed, and as the venerable St. Paul's Cathedral went up in flames, melted lead from the ancient church dome ran in streams down the hillside to the Thames.

Christopher Wren presented Charles with an elaborate plan for rebuilding the city with wide boulevards and open squares, but a lack of funds and haggling over property rights doomed the ambitious project. Wren was able to carry out his plans for rebuilding St. Paul's Cathedral and 52 other churches across the city. New residential areas were laid out for the aristocracy.

Charles II's marriage in 1662 to Catherine of Braganza, the daughter of the King of Portugal, opened up the Far East to English trade and brought about the introduction of tea to the English. After a series of miscarriages, it became clear that the marriage would produce no heir. In 1670, an anxious Parliament passed legislation expanding the grounds for a royal divorce and pressed Charles to divorce Catherine, but the King refused, which meant his brother James would likely succeed him. This caused great concern in England because James remained a stridently unrepentant Catholic. James had been raised as a Catholic by his mother, Queen Henrietta Maria, while the family was in exile in the court of Louis XIV.

Although Charles II joked that he had little need for guards since there was no one in the kingdom who would kill him and make James king, rumors spread of pro-Catholic plots. It was claimed that the Great Fire had been started by Catholics. In fact, Charles had secretly entered into a treaty with his brother-in-law, Louis XIV, promising to restore England to Catholicism in exchange for covert loans.

Two parties fought for power within Charles II's Parliament, the pro-Royalist Tories and the Whigs, who sought to restrict the power of the crown and to exclude James from succession. Parliament enacted the Test Act of 1673, which barred Catholics from high office, forcing James to step down from his post as Lord High Admiral. When the Whig-dominated Parliament passed the Exclusion Bill, attempting to bar James from the throne, Charles dissolved Parliament in 1681.

Charles II died of chronic renal failure in February 1685. (Some historians believe he may have been poisoned.) On his deathbed, he apologized for "taking so long a-dying." After James cleared the King's bedroom of witnesses, he slipped in a Catholic priest, and Charles secretly received last rites on his deathbed.

Resistance in Parliament to James II's succession was overcome as James quickly put down an attempt to place Charles II's illegitimate son, the Protestant Duke of Monmouth, on the throne. The stubborn and arrogant James had learned nothing from the execution of his father or the struggles of his brother, and became even more militantly Catholic. He appointed only Roman Catholics as army officers and dismissed the Bishop of London. When Parliament objected to these actions in 1685, James dissolved Parliament and raised a large, standing army, which he threateningly quartered near London. In 1688, James signed the Declaration of Indulgence restoring all rights to Catholics. Protestors, including seven Bishops, were jailed, uniting Tories and many Whigs against the King.

James's first wife, Anne Hyde, had given him two daughters, Mary and Anne, who had both been raised as Protestants. During the reign of Charles II, Mary had been wed to the Dutch Prince, William of Orange, the champion of the Protestant cause on the continent. After his wife's death, James married the Catholic Italian princess Mary Beatrice of Modena. Mary gave birth to a healthy baby boy, which raised the specter of a Catholic successor. Fears of a conspiracy were inflamed because James had foolishly allowed only Catholic witnesses to be present at the birth. It was widely rumored that the healthy baby boy had been smuggled into Mary's chamber in a warming pan.

The painful memories of the bloody Civil War and the chaos of the Protectorate were still fresh in the minds of the English. Many had hoped that eventually the crown would pass to one of James's Protestant daughters, but now the birth of a healthy baby boy—a Catholic heir—was the final straw. In 1688, the Bishop of London and six prominent Members of the House of Lords joined in an open invitation to the Protestant Prince William of Orange to rescue England. He was asked to depose James, so that his wife, Mary (James's eldest daughter), could ascend to the throne.

When William landed with his army, he was enthusiastically received by the people. James soon found he had few followers. Even his stalwart general John Churchill (the future Duke of Marlborough) had defected. James panicked and threw the Great Seal of England into the Thames as he fled London seeking refuge in the court of France's King Louis XIV. James made only one half-hearted attempt to regain the throne, but his French and Irish soldiers were decisively routed at the Battle of Boyne in Ireland. James died in exile in 1701.

House of Orange and Stuart (1689-1702)

Parliament had hoped that Mary, as the rightful heir to the throne, would rule as Queen with William acting as King Consort so that her sister Anne could succeed if William and Mary had no surviving children. The prideful William of Orange refused to serve as mere Consort and would not agree to step aside in favor of his sister-in-law. When Mary stood by her husband, Parliament gave in.

In 1689, William III and Mary II were allowed to take the throne as co-rulers—the only time in its long history that England has been governed by co-equal monarchs. The power of government was fundamentally shifted from the monarch to Parliament when the Declaration of Rights and the Bill of Rights were enacted, restricting the power of the monarch and guaranteeing the rights of Parliament against the monarch's arbitrary rule. The crown was forbidden to levy taxes or maintain a standing army in peacetime without Parliament's consent. Government ministers were subject to Parliamentary approval, and judges could not be removed by the king. Succession to the throne would no longer be based solely on hereditary right, but could be altered by Parliament.

Like Richard I before him, William was a soldier who cared little for governing, and saw England merely as a ready source of cash to fund his wars against the French Catholic King Louis XIV, his sworn enemy. Although he allowed his ministers and Parliament to run the country, popular resentment grew against their absentee king.

Queen Mary suffered a succession of miscarriages and stillbirths. After ruling only five years, Mary died of smallpox in 1694. During her short reign, she became much loved—perhaps because her sunny nature made it easier for her subjects to put up with her dour husband. William continued to reign in his own right for eight more years.

The Act of Settlement in 1701 established the line of succession after William and ensured that only a Protestant would sit on the throne. Under the terms of the act, following William, Princess Anne (Mary's sister) would be the next ruler, followed by Anne's descendants. The throne could then pass to any of William's descendants (but he left none). Finally, the throne would pass to Princess Sophia of Hanover (granddaughter of James I and niece of Charles I), or to her descendants who were Protestant.

In 1702, William was thrown to the ground while out riding near Hampton Court, when his horse stumbled over a molehill. William broke his collarbone and later died from pneumonia. In accordance with the Act of Settlement, Mary's sister Anne took the throne.

House of Stuart (1702-1714)

The reign of the last Stuart monarch saw a further expansion of England's commercial and military power. England declared war against France and intervened in the War of Spanish Succession, winning a series of major victories. In 1704, Britain seized Gibraltar from Spain. The military successes of Anne's reign were due in large part to the skill of John Churchill, whose wife, Sarah Churchill, was Queen Anne's dear friend and closest confidant. The Queen made Churchill the Duke of Marlborough, and he was given funds to build the palace named for his greatest victory—the Battle of Blenheim. Their London residence—the Marlborough House—was built next door to St. James's Palace across from the Friary Court.

Sarah grew overbearing and even berated the Queen in public. As favorites of the monarch had discovered before her, royal patronage can be withdrawn. In 1710, Sarah was stripped of her offices, and her husband, the Duke of Marlborough, was removed as commander of the British army.

Throughout her reign Anne was sickly. Today, it is believed she suffered from the blood disease, porphyria, which was later to plague George III. Anne married Prince George of Denmark and carried seventeen children, but many miscarried. Only her son William lived until age 11. She suffered so terribly from gout and rheumatism that she had to be carried to her coronation. Anne had to be taken about in a wheelchair and grew so corpulent that at her death, her coffin was almost square.

Anne's reign saw the creation of Great Britain by fully uniting England and Scotland in the Act of Union in 1707. Ireland did not join the Union until 1801. Tea and coffee houses became fashionable gathering places. The South Sea Trading Company expanded its trade to South America. Toward the end of her life, Anne tried in vain to convince her half-brother, James, to renounce Catholicism and return to England to carry on the Stuart line, but he refused to abandon his faith. Anne disliked Sophia of Hanover, but in the end agreed to abide by the Act of Settlement. In 1714, Anne died at age 49. Sophia, who had stood next in line to the throne, had died from a stroke just two months earlier and so the throne passed to Sophia's 54-year-old son George.

House of Hanover (1741-1901)

George ascended the throne as George I, even though there were over 50 descendants more closely related by blood to the Stuart dynasty. They were bypassed to ensure that only a Protestant would sit on the throne. The people did not care much for their thoroughly German King, but preferred him as the lesser of two evils over the so-called "James III," the Catholic heir to the House of Stuart. George's accession was immediately challenged by James III, also known as the "Old Pretender," but the Stuart army was routed in Scotland, even before James arrived. He fled to France, where his patron, Louis IV, died in 1715, leaving England to enjoy years of peace and growing prosperity.

The old aristocracy viewed the influx of new German courtiers with alarm when George arrived in London with his entourage of German retainers and mistresses–but without his wife. Years before his accession to the throne, George's wife, Sophia, had been imprisoned for life when she was discovered having an affair with a Swedish Colonel. The new King loved music. George Frederick Handel had been George I's court musician in Hanover and he came to London, where he enjoyed a successful career. The King founded the first Royal Academy of Music in 1720.

George never bothered to learn English and spent much of his reign visiting his former home in Hanover. Because of George I's unfamiliarity with English culture and politics, the government was left to his cabinet of ministers. George grew to rely so heavily on Robert Walpole, his First Lord of the Treasury, that Walpole was regarded by many as the King's "prime minister." Walpole detested the term, which he considered derogatory, but his role as liaison between the Crown and Parliament forged the position of Prime Minister that has continued until this day. George I eventually alienated Walpole, who allied himself with the King's son and heir, George Augustus. George I died in 1727 at age 67 and was buried in Hanover.

George II was 30 when his father took the throne and had an opportunity to learn more about the English before he was crowned. The young George never forgave his father for his mother's lifelong imprisonment for adultery. After a heated argument with his father in 1717, the young prince, banished from St. James's Palace, set up a rival court-in-waiting and worked with Robert Walpole to undermine his father's policies.

George II was utterly devoted to his wife, Caroline of Ansbach, who bore him three sons and five daughters and came to wield a powerful influence on the King. Caroline helped Walpole keep his position as Prime Minister until he finally retired in 1742. George was a passionate military man, eager for foreign intervention, but, with the Queen's support, Walpole managed to keep the country out of war for the first twelve years of George II's reign. When Caroline died in 1737, it became impossible for Walpole to restrain the King. Without Caroline's moderating influence, war was inevitable. Deaf to Walpole's pleas, George II declared war on Spain in 1739 in the so-called War of Jenkin's Ear. An English sea captain, Jenkins, had his ear cut off in a skirmish with the Spanish forces, which claimed he was caught smuggling—but the supposed "provocation" had occurred some eight years earlier. The real cause was the growing commercial rivalry between England and Spain in the New World.

The fighting quickly became entangled in the complex War of Austrian Succession, in which the European powers struggled to determine who would inherit the Hapsburg throne. Battles raged across Europe, the

Americas, and even in India. When French forces threatened Hanover, George II (who was nearly 60 at the time) bravely led his army in the Battle of Dettingen. He was the last British King to personally lead troops into battle.

In 1745, Prince Charles Edward Stuart (grandson of James II), known as the "Young Pretender" and "Bonnie Prince Charlie," led the last Jacobite rebellion to restore the Stuart dynasty. His small army landed in Scotland but was wiped out in the bloody Battle of Culloden Moor. Bonnie Prince Charlie, disguised as the maid to his supporter, Flora MacDonald, escaped to France and later made his way to Italy, where he drank himself to death in Rome in 1789.

In 1756, England declared war on France. In the Seven Years War, the struggle between Great Britain and France (and later, Spain) spilled over to North America, where it is known as the French and Indian War. In 1759, British forces led by General James Wolfe captured Quebec and the French were expelled from Canada. In 1757, the East India Company, led by Robert Clive, gave Britain control of India in the Battle of Plassey. British forces made further territorial gains in Africa and the West Indies as the British Empire expanded.

George II died of a stroke in 1760 at the age of 77. His son, Frederick Louis, Prince of Wales, had died in 1751, having never ruled, and so George II was succeeded by his 22-year-old grandson, George III. George III was the first Hanoverian King to be born in London and to speak English as his native tongue. In a speech in 1760 he declared, "Born and educated in this country, I glory in the name of Briton." He married Charlotte of Mecklenberg-Strelitz shortly before his coronation. George was determined to regain the power that had seeped away during the reigns of his grandfather and great-grandfather. His desire to strengthen the prerogatives and authority of the monarch was frustrated by the war debt he inherited, the revolt of the American colonies, and later his recurring bouts with porphyria, a blood disease, which resulted in the famous "Madness of King George."

The Seven Years War was finally concluded by the Peace of Paris, signed in 1763, under which France ceded Canada and all its territories east of the Mississippi River to England, and Spain gave up its claims to Florida. The treaty firmly established the British Empire and recognized its maritime supremacy. One unforeseen consequence was that the enormous cost of the war forced Parliament to levy taxes on its American colonies, which had long enjoyed freedom from taxation.

George III's first Prime Minister, the heavy-handed John Stuart, Earl of Bute, introduced new taxes to retire the war debt. Bute became so hated by colonists and the British people that he was forced to resign after only eleven months in office. He was followed by a succession of weak ministers until Lord North was appointed in 1770. When North introduced a tea tax in 1773, a group of colonists dressed as Indians dumped a cargo of British tea into Boston harbor in the so-called Boston Tea Party. The British closed the port and sent troops in to restore order.

George III.

In 1774, the first Continental Congress met in Philadelphia to discuss their grievances. The following year colonial forces clashed with the British troops in the Battle of Lexington. The representatives of the colonies proclaimed their independence on July 4, 1776. The King was stunned when British General John Burgoyne was forced to surrender his army in the battle of Saratoga in 1777. The surprise victory won new respect abroad for the colonial forces. France, eager to strike back at her old nemesis, supported the colonies' war effort. When General Cornwallis surrendered at Yorktown in 1781, Britain was finally forced to recognize American independence. The Peace of Versailles was signed in 1783. Lord North resigned in disgrace. George could never comprehend why the British colonies had been lost and refused to have the subject even mentioned in his presence.

Despite the loss of the American colonies, George III's rule brought relative stability in England during a time when chaos raged in Europe. The French monarchy was abolished in September, 1791. King Louis XVI's execution in 1793 was followed by the terrors of the French Revolution and the rise of Napoleon. By 1797, French armies led by Napoleon dominated the European continent. In May of 1804, Napoleon was proclaimed Emperor. Panic spread as the nation desperately looked across the English Channel at Napoleon's gathering invasion force. Two able soldiers, Lord Horatio Nelson and Arthur Wellesley, the Duke of Wellington, emerged to rescue Britain from Napoleon's menace.

Led by Lord Horatio Nelson, the British navy defeated the combined French and Spanish naval forces off the coast of Spain in the Battle of Trafalgar in October 1805, ending the threat of invasion. Britain declared war against the United States for its support of the French, and captured and burned the American capital at Washington in the War of 1812. Napoleon's domination of Europe ended when the Duke of Wellington defeated his ground forces in the Battle of Waterloo in 1815.

George III's first mental breakdown, caused by the blood disease porphyria, came in 1788. He recovered, but then relapsed in 1801 and again in 1804. By 1810, depressed over the death of his beloved youngest daughter, Amelia, the King finally succumbed to the disease. Rule was formally given to his son George as Prince Regent in 1811. When George III died at Windsor Castle on January 29, 1820, he was blind, deaf, and completely insane. Despite the turmoil on the continent and the King's health, George III's reign saw prosperity flourish in Britain. The use of the new steam engine powering spinning machines ignited a revolution in the British textile industry. There was a blossoming of literature with the works of William Wordsworth, Percy Shelley, and Lord Byron.

Relations between the King and his son, George Augustus Frederick, were always strained. The vain young heir was an insatiable womanizer. After a series of mistresses, the young prince secretly married Maria Fitzherbert, a twice-widowed Catholic six years his senior, when she refused to become his mistress. The Act of Settlement of 1701 prohibited a British heir to the throne's marriage to a Catholic, and the Royal Marriages Act of 1772 forbade any royal marriage without the approval of the King and Privy Council. The King was outraged and promptly annulled the clandestine marriage.

After the young prince ran up enormous debts, his father and Parliament offered to settle his debts if the profligate prince would marry his cousin, Princess Caroline of Brunswick. Reluctantly, the cash-strapped George agreed. When George first set eyes on his homely cousin, he fainted. He was married in a drunken haze at the Chapel Royal in St. James's Palace and passed out on his wedding night. Even so, the heir apparent performed his duty to God and Country. Nine months later their only child, Charlotte Augusta, was born. Shortly thereafter, the couple separated. Caroline took off to the continent, where she was romantically linked with Bartolomeo

Pergami, an Italian courtier.

When King George III died, Caroline rushed back to London to take her place as Queen. George IV had Parliament launch an inquiry into Caroline's romantic affairs. Caroline threatened to reveal George's prior secret marriage to the Catholic Maria Fitzherbert. As his coronation approached, George even offered to pay her to go away, but she refused. George had Caroline physically barred when she tried to force her way in to attend his elaborate coronation ceremony at Westminster Abbey. Stunned by the public humiliation, Caroline died three weeks later of intestinal blockage.

George IV.

In his nine years serving as Regent during his father's periods of mental infirmity and his ten years as King, George was a compulsive spender, builder, and collector. Many of the most extravagant works of art and decorative items in the Royal Collection on display in the Queen's Gallery and Windsor Castle were acquired during this "Regency" period of dazzling high society. The Royal Pavilion at Brighton was rebuilt in an elaborate Oriental style by George IV's favorite architect, John Nash, whose handiwork can also be seen in Regent's Park, Regent's Street, and the Carlton House. Nash undertook to rebuild Buckingham Palace as a showplace for the King, but work was hampered by a chronic shortage of funds from the King's many other grand building schemes.

In 1828, King George IV called upon the elderly war hero, the Duke of Wellington, to serve as his Prime Minister as he fought to squelch political reform. In 1829, the Catholic Relief Act was passed, which allowed Catholics to serve in the Parliament. George died at Windsor Castle in 1830 at age 67. His only daughter, Charlotte Augusta, had died in childbirth and so the crown passed to George IV's 64-year-old brother, who was crowned William IV.

William, the third son of George III, had never expected to take the throne. He joined the navy at 14 and had served under Lord Nelson in the

West Indies. William had many very public affairs until he settled down in unmarried bliss with actress Dorothea Jordan for some twenty years, producing ten illegitimate children. When George IV's heir died in childbirth, William stood next in line to the throne. The 54-year-old William was quickly married to the 25-year-old Princess Adelaide of Saxe-Mieningen in the hopes of producing an heir. She bore him two daughters, but neither survived infancy.

William was miserly, and his explosive rages were legendary. Nicknamed the "Sailor King" for his nautical past or "Silly Billy" for his very public tantrums, he luckily had the advice of good ministers. He grudgingly allowed the passage of the Reform Act of 1832, which extended the right to vote to half a million more citizens, and began the more equitable redistribution of seats in Parliament. In 1833, slavery was abolished in the British Empire. The Factory Act forbade children under 9 from working in factories and those under 13 from working more than 48 hours a week. The misguided Poor Law Act of 1834 created workhouses for the poor, which were scathingly derided by Charles Dickens's 1837 *Oliver Twist*. William died of pneumonia and cirrhosis of the liver on June 20, 1837, leaving his young niece, Princess Alexandrina Victoria (the daughter of the Duke of Kent, George III's deceased fourth son) to succeed him as Queen.

Victoria came to the throne at 18 years of age when public respect for monarchy was at low ebb. After the extravagance and moral decadence of

George IV and the lackluster reign of the obstructionist William IV, many people saw little point in continuing with the monarchy. During the first four years of her reign there were three assassination attempts. Her first year was rocked with scandal when the Queen expelled her Lady-in-Waiting, Lady Flora Hastings, whom the Queen believed was pregnant out of wedlock. Lady Flora denied any affair, but she was ordered to leave her position. She was later found to have cancer of the liver and her death brought public scorn on the new monarch, who was heckled and booed

Queen Victoria.

when she went to the races at Ascot.

Victoria fell in love with her cousin, the young German Prince Albert of Saxe-Coburg-Gotha, when they met in 1836, and asked Albert to marry her on their second meeting in 1839. They were married on February 10, 1840, in the Chapel Royal at St. James's Palace, when they were both 20. She gave him nine children.

Sir Robert Peel became Prime Minister in 1841 and won the Queen's respect. She reluctantly gave her blessing to Britain's participation with France in the ill-fated Crimean War against Russia.

As Albert pushed for more power for

The ornate Albert Memorial.

the Queen, Victoria's subjects viewed her husband with increasing distrust and resented his "German" ways. Albert was not even named Prince Consort until after seventeen years of marriage. Albert believed the Royal Family should set an example of moral rectitude for the nation, and he sternly ruled the royal household.

Sincerely concerned over the welfare of the British people, Albert planned and spearheaded the Great Exhibition of 1851, which served as a showcase for British innovations in technology. In effect, it was the first World's Fair. The centerpiece of the Great Exhibition and the engineering marvel of the age was the Crystal Palace, a gigantic, prefabricated, steel and glass structure erected in Hyde Park to house the exhibits. The Exhibition was a huge success, with over 17,000 exhibitors from as far away as China and over six million visitors. The profit was used to create the Victoria and Albert Museum.

Albert's sudden death from typhoid in 1861 left the Queen devastated. Inconsolable, the "Widow of Windsor" withdrew from public view and carried out her duties through her ministers. The grief-stricken Queen went into seclusion and did not return to public life until the final 20 years of her reign. The romantic antics of her son, the Prince of Wales, brought further dissatisfaction with the monarchy. Scandalous rumors flew over the relationship between the Queen and John Brown, a Scottish manservant of her late husband, Prince Albert. Newspapers referred to the Queen as "Mrs. Brown."

After years of the Queen's absence from the public stage, there were many calls for her abdication. Her new Prime Minister, Benjamin Disraeli, coaxed her out of her self-imposed exile in 1874 and, to her delight, engineered Victoria's additional title as "Empress of India" in 1876. Disraeli twice served as Victoria's Prime Minister, and she grew to be quite fond of him. The Queen's relations were far chillier with William E. Gladstone, who served four times as her Prime Minister.

The last years of Victoria's reign were strained by friction between Ireland and Britain over Home Rule—whether the Irish should be allowed to rule themselves—and by the British losses in the Boer War in South Africa. But by the time of her Golden Jubilee in 1887, and then her Diamond Jubilee in 1897, Queen Victoria had grown to be the adored symbol of the British Empire. Through her many children she was related by blood or marriage to almost all of the royal families in Europe. When Victoria died at 81 on January 22, 1901, her record 64-year reign had seen a transformation of British society. The British Empire reached its apex as the world's dominant military and commercial power. Truly the sun never set on the Union Jack, which ruled over a quarter of the world's population around the globe.

House Saxe-Coburg-Gotha (1901-1910)

Edward VII had waited 59 years before he took the throne. Victoria blamed Edward's affair with an actress for aggravating the illness of her dear Albert, who later succumbed to typhoid. The Queen never forgave him and prevented Edward from taking any part in affairs of state. Edward responded by indulging himself with wine, food, beautiful women, and gambling. Edward was a society darling. Whether racing horses at Ascot, hunting big game in Africa, or gambling in Monte Carlo, the portly Edward set the tone for the "Edwardian Age." Edward grew so corpulent he was lampooned in the press as "the Prince of Whales."

In 1863, Edward married Princess Alexandra of Denmark, who turned a blind eye to Edward's very public dalliances with women, particularly the Countess of Warwick, actress Lillie Langtry, and Mrs. Alice Keppel, who held on to the King's affection until his death. Queen Alexandra was devoted to her philandering husband and their six children, which endeared her to the people.

Edward ruled for only ten years, but he was hailed as "The

Peacemaker" and was instrumental in forming the Triple Entente among England, France, and Italy. Through his mother's extensive family relations, Edward was seen as the uncle of Europe in the halcyon days before the First World War would turn their privileged world upside down. Edward died at Buckingham Palace on May 6, 1910. After the King's death, Queen Alexandra lived out her days in the seclusion of the Marlborough House until her death in 1925.

House of Windsor (1910-the present)

George V.

George V, the King's second son, was rather shy. Like William IV, he was trained for a career in the navy and never expected to take the throne. George had little formal education and is thought never to have read a single book as an adult. A man of simple tastes, he was fond of shooting and stamp collecting. His naval career ended upon the death of his elder brother in 1892, when he became heir to the throne. In 1893, he married his late brother's fiancée, Princess Mary of Teck, who became his devoted helpmate. They had five sons and a daughter.

George and Mary were crowned together at Westminster Abbey on June 22, 1911. They were also crowned in New Delhi as Emperor and Empress of India, which neither his grandmother Victoria or father Edward VII had chosen to do. George reigned for only three years before the assassination of Archduke Ferdinand in Sarajevo on June 28, 1914 plunged the world into the horrors of the First World War. George was placed in the awkward position of being at war with his first cousin, Kaiser Wilhelm II, Emperor of Germany. Both were grandchildren of Queen Victoria.

The King did his best to keep up British morale, visiting the troops and sharing in the public rationing. In 1917 George declared that the Royal Family, formerly known as the House of Saxe-Coburg-Gotha (from his father Prince Albert), would take the name of the House of Windsor, and he renounced all German titles and names.

George was shocked when his cousin Nicholas, Tsar of Russia, was forced to abdicate. Nicholas pleaded with his cousin to allow the Russian Royal Family refuge in England, but on the advice of his ministers, George declined. At first the revolution in Russia was seen as a clash between the autocrats and the oppressed common people, and George feared a possible anti-monarchist backlash from his own people. He was later overcome with grief and guilt when Nicholas and his entire family were murdered in 1918.

Queen Mary won praise for her tireless efforts in personally tending to wounded soldiers. She also was instrumental in rearranging and organizing the vast Royal Collection of art and antiques.

Britain was rocked with social unrest and labor strikes following the end of the "War to End All Wars." Women fought for the right to vote with sometimes violent demonstrations, chaining themselves to railings outside Parliament and going on hunger strikes in jail. After years of the Suffragette movement, the 1918 Reform Act finally extended the right to vote to women, but only to those over thirty years of age. The following year, Lady Astor became the first woman to take a seat in the House of Commons. It was not until 1928 that the right to vote was finally given on an equal basis to all men and women over the age of twenty-one.

For years the Protestant population in Northern Ireland had been fighting against domination by the Catholic majority in the south. In 1920-21, Ireland was partitioned into the province of Northern Ireland for Protestants and the southern free state for Catholics. The slow breakup of the British Empire began with the 1931 Statute of Westminster, which recognized the independence of the former colonies and formally changed the British Empire into the Commonwealth. The King remained the titular head of the Commonwealth, but control of the overseas dominions by Parliament ended.

George V made his first radio broadcast on Christmas day in 1932. It was the first time many of his subjects had ever heard their King. The reassuring voice of the old King brought comfort and a sense of stability through the Great Depression. In January 1936, the King fell critically ill while at Windsor Castle. Recently it has been revealed that near midnight on January 20th, the royal physician administered a fatal injection of cocaine and morphine to ease the King's suffering—and to ensure that the King's death notice would appear in the first edition of *The Times*.

The King was succeeded by his eldest son, the future Edward VIII, known in the family as David. Before his father died, David had fallen in love with Mrs. Wallis Simpson, an American, who had divorced her first husband and was in the process of divorcing her second. When the media scandal over her relationship with the Prince of Wales surfaced, the future of the monarchy was thrown into a profound crisis. Mrs. Simpson's second divorce would be finalized only two weeks before the coronation. The Archbishop of Canterbury and Edward's mother, Queen Mary, were dead set against the

The Duke and Duchess of Windsor following Edward VIII's abdication.

marriage, for the King would be the Head of the Church of England. Undeterred, Edward was determined to bully his way through. Edward delivered an ultimatum to Prime Minister Stanley Baldwin that he would either marry Wallis or renounce the throne. Edward's strategy failed. His Prime Minister stood fast, telling Edward the people would never accept the marriage.

Edward renounced his claim to the throne. In his radio address to the nation Edward explained he had chosen to abdicate rather than give up "the help and support of the woman I love." Edward later was made Duke of Windsor, but his wife was denied the title of "Royal Highness."

Edward caused outrage when he and Wallis visited Germany and met with Hitler in 1937. Edward was sent during WWII to serve as Governor to the Bahamas—far from the reach of German forces who might use him as a puppet ruler after an invasion of Britain. After the war, Edward spent the last years of his life in Paris, remaining distanced from the Royal Family, even though Queen Elizabeth II visited him shortly before his death in 1972 at the age of 77. Wallis lived until 90 and was buried at Windsor Castle beside her husband of 35 years. Recently it has been revealed that, while Edward was considering renouncing the throne to marry her, Wallis was secretly carrying on an affair with Guy Trundle, a married car salesman, whom she showered with gifts and cash.

Edward's younger brother, known in the Royal Family as Bertie, had avoided public duties because he stuttered. He had married a commoner, Lady Elizabeth Bowes-Lyon, in 1923 and they had two young daughters, Elizabeth, born in 1926, and Margaret, born in 1930. Bertie had never expected to be king, but the painfully shy naval officer found himself thrust into the limelight upon the abdication of his brother, Edward VIII.

George VI Coronation shown *(left to right)* Queen Elizabeth, George VI *(foreground)* Princesses Elizabeth and Margaret.

He was crowned as George VI at Westminster Abbey on May 12, 1937, while the threat of Nazi aggression loomed on the horizon. Prime Minister Stanley Baldwin resigned and was replaced by Neville Chamberlain, who sought to avoid war by pursuing a policy of appeasement with Hitler. In 1939, Hitler invaded Czechoslovakia and then Poland, Norway, and the Netherlands. With the fall of France, German forces were at Britain's doorstep. Retreating British troops were evacuated from the shores of France at Dunkirk.

At George VI's request, Winston Churchill stepped in to replace Chamberlain in 1940. Churchill promised the British people that he "had nothing to offer but blood, toil, tears and sweat." The introverted King was supported by his loving wife Elizabeth and the unconquerable Churchill as the nation struggled through the dark days of the Blitz (from the German word *blitzkrieg*: "lightning war"). It began on September 7, 1940, and for the next 57 consecutive nights, German bombs rained down on London. Some 43,000 civilians were killed in the Battle of Britain and 61,000 were injured. Over 1.25 million homes in the London area were destroyed. The King refused to evacuate his children to Canada and sent them to Windsor Castle. The King stayed in Buckingham Palace throughout the Blitz with his Queen, who famously remarked, "The children won't go without me. I won't leave the King. And the King will never leave."

The King and Queen toured bombed-out sections of London and visited troops and factories across England, boosting morale. When

The Royal Family with Sir Winston Churchill on the balcony of Buckingham Palace.

Buckingham Palace was finally hit in the bombardment, the Queen said she felt she could finally "look the East End in the face." When touring the bomb damage one day, a subject shouted out, "You're a good King!" George replied, "You're a good people." The timid King became a symbol of courage for his beleaguered countrymen.

The United States finally entered the war after the Japanese bombed Pearl Harbor on December 6, 1941. American troops and armaments flowed into England. In 1944, the D-Day landings in Normandy began to drive back the German army as the Soviet Union hammered the Nazis from the east. When the war in Europe ended in 1945, the Royal Family appeared on the balcony of Buckingham Palace with Winston Churchill in the victory celebration, cheered by thousands, as support for the monarchy reached its all-time high in modern times.

After over six years of war, the British people, weary of war and the deprivations of wartime rationing, dismissed Churchill and the Conservatives from power, robbing him of his well-deserved triumph. The newly elected Labour Party, with Clement Attlee as Prime Minister, set out on a program to nationalize the coal, gas, electricity, iron and steel industries. In 1947, India and Pakistan were granted independence. Churchill returned as Prime Minister in 1951. The King's health deteriorated after his left lung was removed due to lung cancer. He died peacefully on February 6, 1952. Princess Elizabeth and her husband were away on goodwill tour on behalf of the ailing King. They were staying at the Treetops Hotel in Kenya when the unexpected news came that Elizabeth's father had suddenly died. She hurried back to London.

Elizabeth had met the charming Philip (a distant cousin) while he was a cadet at the Dartmouth Naval College. His grandfather had been asked to take the vacant throne of Greece, but was later banished by a military coup in 1922. His father, Prince Andrew of Greece and Denmark, was the grandson of King Christian IX of Denmark, and his mother, Princess Alice of Battenberg, was the daughter of Prince Louis of Battenberg. Raised by his uncle, Lord Mountbatten, Philip had served in the Royal Navy during WWII. When it became clear that he was planning to marry the future

Coronation portrait of Queen Elizabeth II.

Queen, he changed his name, renounced any claim to the Greek throne, and became a naturalized British citizen.

Elizabeth and Philip were married on November 20, 1947, at Westminster Abbey. King George VI made Philip Duke of Edinburgh and granted his new son-in-law the right to be called "His Royal Highness." The King also made Philip a Knight of the Garter. Elizabeth and Philip have four children: Charles (born November 14, 1948), Anne (born August 15, 1950), Andrew (born February 19, 1960), and Edward (born March 10, 1964). The royal children use the surname Windsor after the Queen's father, George VI, instead of their father's last name, Mountbatten.

Elizabeth was only 25 when she ascended to the throne. She was crowned at Westminster Abbey on June 2, 1953, during a ceremony heard live on radio and, for the first time, televised and broadcast worldwide to an estimated 20 million people. Another million subjects lined the streets of London for the joyful celebration.

The new Queen was determined to use the new medium of television to bring her closer to her people. Her Christmas Day message was broadcast on radio and television beginning in 1957—a tradition that continues today, although the address is now prerecorded so that the Queen can be with her family on Christmas.

Churchill remained her Prime Minister until ill health forced him to step down in 1955. Churchill was succeeded by Anthony Eden, who resigned after Britain and France attempted to seize the Suez Canal in 1956 to prevent Egypt's president, Abdul Nasser, from nationalizing the strategic waterway. Under great pressure from the United States, the Anglo-French forces withdrew. The Queen's eldest son, Prince Charles, was invested as Prince of Wales in 1969, in a live broadcast from Caernarvon Castle, Wales. The same year saw the beginning of the "Troubles" in Northern Ireland with mounting IRA violence against British rule.

Britain joined the European Union in 1973. In 1979, Margaret Thatcher became the first woman to serve as Prime Minister. The "Iron Lady's" record-breaking tenure was marked by social polarization and widespread discontent as unemployment reached three million as she struggled against Britain's out-of-control trade unions to reverse Britain's economic decline. Thatcher's popularity was boosted by the 1982 Falkland War over Argentina's seizure of the Falkland Islands. She held on to her position until she resigned in 1990.

Britain participated with the United States in the Gulf War in 1991 and took part in the peacekeeping missions in Bosnia and Afghanistan. The defeat of the Conservatives brought the new Labour Party to power in 1997. In 2003, Britain, under Prime Minister Tony Blair, joined the United States to oust Saddam Hussein from power in Iraq despite strong public opposition to the war.

Elizabeth II's Silver Jubilee, celebrated in 1977, was followed by the turbulent final decades of the 20th century. In 1974, a gunman tried to abduct Princess Anne as she and her first husband, Captain Mark Phillips, were being driven along the Mall. In 1979, Earl Mountbatten of Burma, Charles's great-uncle, was murdered when the IRA blew up his fishing boat. While the Queen was riding in the 1981 Trooping the Color, 17-year-old Marcus Sarjeant stepped out from the audience and fired six shots directly at the Queen. Fortunately, the gun was loaded with blanks. Stunned, but unhurt, the Queen went on with the ceremony. The following year the Queen awoke to find a mentally disturbed man, Michael Fagan, sitting at the foot of her bed. She calmly kept the intruder occupied in conversation for over ten minutes until security finally arrived.

Elizabeth's reign has been marked by intense media focus on personal difficulties within the Royal Family. In 1955, the Queen's younger sister,

The Royal Family gathered to watch the 1985 Trooping the Color fly-by.

Princess Margaret, fell in love with Group Captain Peter Townsend, the Queen's Equerry, but he was divorced. In light of Edward VIII's abdication over his proposed marriage to a divorceé, Margaret was convinced public opinion would be against such a match and so she married Antony Armstrong-Jones (made Lord Snowden) in 1960. The couple had two children, David and Sarah (now Viscount Linley, and Lady Sarah Chatto), before the couple divorced in 1978.

Princess Anne, the Queen's only daughter, was given the title "Princess Royal" by the Queen in 1987. In 1973, she married Mark Phillips, then a Lieutenant in the Queen's Dragoon Guards, who was offered, but declined, a title. Before their marriage dissolved in 1992, they had two children, Peter Phillips and Zara Phillips. In December of 1992, Princess Anne married Captain Timothy Laurence of the Royal Navy.

Prince Andrew married Sarah Ferguson—popularly known as "Fergie"—in July of 1986 and was made the Duke of York, Earl of Inverness, and Baron of Killyleagh. Sarah became the Duchess of York. Their marriage unraveled in lurid detail heralded in the London tabloids. They separated in 1992 and were divorced in 1996. They share joint custody of their children, Princess Beatrice of York and Princess Eugenie of York.

Prince Edward graduated from Cambridge in 1986 and spent three years in the Royal Marines before pursuing his interest in theater. He joined

Andrew Lloyd Webber's Really Useful Theatre Company and later formed his own television production company, Ardent Productions, in 1993. Prince Charles was said to be "incandescent with rage" when Edward's company aired footage of Prince William at St. Andrews University after the other media had agreed to give the young prince his privacy. On June 19, 1999, Edward married Sophie Rhys-Jones in a ceremony at St. George's Chapel at Windsor Castle. He was made Earl of Wessex and Viscount Severn, and Sophie became Countess of Wessex.

Princess Diana and Prince Charles on their wedding day.

The greatest blow to the prestige of the British monarchy in recent times came from the ill-fated marriage of Prince Charles to Lady Diana Spencer. An estimated one billion TV viewers watched their lavish, fairytale wedding on July 29, 1981, held at St. Paul's Cathedral (Diana felt Westminster Abbey was too small).

Prince Andrew and his wife Sarah Ferguson on their wedding day.

Diana was unable to cope with the pressures of living in the royal fishbowl under the continuous glare of the insatiable tabloid press. Charles found he had little in common with his young, modern bride and sought comfort from his longtime mistress, Camilla Parker-Bowles, who shared Charles's passions for country life and horses. Princess Diana turned to others as

Prince Edward and wife Sophie Rhys-Jones, after their wedding at St. George's Chapel in Windsor Castle.

The Prince and Princess of Wales and their sons Prince William *(right)* and Prince Harry *(left)*.

well. Despite their marital difficulties, Charles and Diana were able to do their duty to provide an "heir and a spare" to continue the House of Windsor. Before their marriage disintegrated in the "War of the Wales," they had two sons, Prince William Arthur Philip Louis (known as William) born on June 21, 1982, and Prince Henry Charles Albert David (known as Harry) born September 15, 1984. After separating in 1992, Diana gave up her title of Her Royal Highness and was known as Diana, Princess of Wales. She remained at Kensington Palace, while Charles stayed at St. James's Palace and Highgrove in nearby Gloucestershire.

Queen Elizabeth called 1992 her *annus horribilis* (horrible year), which she described in her understated way as "not a year I look back on with undiluted pleasure." Fire had swept through Windsor Castle in November of 1992. Her daughter Princess Anne had divorced. The marriages of Prince Charles to Diana, and Prince Edward to Sarah Ferguson had ended in a media feeding frenzy. That same year the Queen bowed to public pressure and agreed to pay income taxes on her private revenue and to make the Prince of Wales' revenue from the Duchy of Cornwall taxable. To raise funds for the renovation of Windsor Castle, Buckingham Palace was opened to the public.

In a television interview in 1994, Prince Charles admitted to adultery. This was followed by the retaliatory confession by Diana who told the worldwide audience, "There were three of us in this marriage, so it was a bit crowded." To end the public backbiting, the Queen consented to Charles and Diana's divorce in 1996. Diana was killed the following year in an appalling car crash in Paris with Emad "Dodi" Fayed, the son of billionaire businessman Mohamed Al-Fayed. The public outrage at

Funeral of Princess Diana at Westminster Abbey.

the Queen's stoic reaction brought calls for the abolition of the monarchy. Many suggested the crown should bypass Prince Charles. The Royal Family was stunned by the overwhelming show of public grief following Diana's death. A worldwide audience watched the funeral on September 6, 1997, at Westminster Abbey. The Princess was laid to rest at her family's estate at Althorp.

With his mother's striking looks and his father's keen intellect, young Prince William has tried to satisfy the demands of royal duties and the media's interest in him as future king, while fending off the intrusion of the media into his personal affairs, which wreaked such havoc in his late mother's life. When he turned eighteen, he asked the Queen that his title "His Royal Highness" be postponed, and yet he was the first Royal to be featured on a set of stamps, which were released for his 21st birthday in 2003. He graduated from Eton College in 2000 and spent a year working on conservation and community projects in Belize and Chile, and later spent time in Africa. In 2001, he began studying Art

Prince Harry and Prince William.

Three generations of the Royal Family at Westminster Abbey in June 2003 to mark the 50th anniversary of the Queen's coronation.

History at St. Andrew's University in Scotland.

Outgoing and handsome, Prince Harry has lived in the shadow of his older brother. He was taken by his father to a drug rehabilitation clinic for a day in 2002 after he admitted smoking marijuana and drinking alcohol. Harry followed his brother William to Eton College where he graduated in 2003. While at Eton, Harry excelled in sports and in the elite school's cadet corps. He applied to Sandhurst military academy (the British equivalent of West Point) where he plans to pursue a military career. Although the media agreed to leave the young princes alone after their mother's tragic death, they will be subjected to increasingly intense press scrutiny as they step out into the world as adults and assume greater public duties.

The death of the Queen's sister, Princess Margaret, on February 9, 2002, followed by the death of the widely adored Queen Mother on March 30, 2002, at the age of 101, produced a wave of sympathy for the long-suffering Queen. The Queen's celebration of her Golden Jubilee in 2002 saw a resurgence of popular support for the Queen. Elizabeth II is now the longest-reigning monarch since Queen Victoria. Only five earlier British monarchs—Henry III, Edward III, James I, George III, and Victoria—have enjoyed fifty years on the throne.

The goodwill generated by her Golden Jubilee was tarnished by the sensational revelations in the trial of

Prince Charles and Camilla Parker-Bowles.

Queen Elizabeth II and the Prince of Wales after the 2002 Trooping the Color.

Princess Diana's former butler, Paul Burrell. The life and tragic death of Princess Diana demonstrated to the Queen and her advisors that her people want a more human face to the monarchy, but the Royal Family has struggled to find the right balance between adherence to tradition and the need to keep pace with changes in society. Given the long life of her mother, the Queen Mum, Queen Elizabeth II's reign may yet challenge the record of Queen Victoria's lengthy reign, which also saw many highs and lows. Over the centuries, the prestige of the monarchy has been buffeted by scandals and rumors, but somehow has managed to survive. Despite the cynics who have predicted that she would be Queen Elizabeth the Last, the genuine outpouring of affection received by the Queen during her recent Golden Jubilee has suggested to many that she has many years left to rule.

She is the 40th monarch since William the Conqueror took the throne in 1066, and can trace her bloodline back to the Saxon King Egbert in A.D. 825. Her steadfast devotion to her duties as Queen and her quiet strength of character have seen the nation through a half-century of rapid, sometimes tumultuous, changes. After two World Wars have swept away most of Europe's monarchies, Queen Elizabeth II still remains as the hardworking head of one of the few constitutional monarchies in the modern world.

CHAPTER 3
THE ROLE OF THE MONARCHY—
WHAT DOES THE QUEEN DO?

The Government

The British Constitution is not embodied in a single document. The United Kingdom is governed under a unique system of constitutional monarchy and parliamentary democracy. Its system of government has evolved over the centuries, and is made up of statutory law (enacted by Parliament), common law (judicial decisions), and unwritten traditions that have been shaped by its distinctive history. Today the Queen's role is primarily symbolic and ceremonial, but her real power is the influence she wields by virtue of her position as monarch and the respect she has earned through years of devoted service to her country since her coronation on June 3, 1953.

While the executive power is nominally vested in the Queen, it is exercised through her cabinet, which is headed by the Prime Minister. After each General Election, the leader of the party that wins a majority of seats in the House of Commons is invited by the Queen to form a new government and serve as her Prime Minister. The Prime Minister selects the other ministers of the new government. The Prime Minister and his ministers manage the departments and committees that oversee the running of the government and propose new laws in the form of bills, which are presented to Parliament for consideration.

Parliament consists of two houses—the House of Commons and the House of Lords. The Members of Parliament, known as "MPs," debate new legislation proposed by the Prime Minister. Legislation concerning taxation and finance is introduced solely in the House of Commons and must be approved by the House of Lords without amendment. Originally the House of Lords could veto legislation, but now the House of Lords may only delay passage of a bill for one year. The House of Lords has traditionally been seen as a check on the power and possible excesses of the House of Commons. Since 1949, only three acts have been passed into law without the consent of the House of Lords.

The House of Lords as an institution is undergoing a historic transition that may well signal future changes for the monarchy. The House of Lords Act of 1999 removed the right of most of the 750 Hereditary Peers to sit and vote in the House of Lords; only 92 Hereditary Peers (74 of whom were elected by their fellow Hereditary Peers) have been allowed to retain their seats and the right to vote in the transitional House of Lords. The matter is currently under vigorous debate in Britain, but the reformers intend to remove the entitlement of the Hereditary Peers to sit in the House of Lords altogether and transform the upper house into a more representational legislative body. In 2003, Prime Minister Tony Blair moved to abolish the 1,400-year-old post of Lord Chancellor. The Lord Chancellor was formerly the chief of the judiciary, a cabinet minister, and the speaker of the House of Lords.

The Duties of the Queen

The Queen's full title is "Queen Elizabeth II, by the Grace of God, Queen of this Realm and of Her other Realms and Territories, Head of the Commonwealth, Defender of the Faith." The Queen serves as the official Head of State of the United Kingdom. The Queen is the Head of the Armed Services and acts as Supreme Governor of the Church of England. She is also nominally the Sovereign of Canada, Australia, and New Zealand, as well as the Commonwealth countries of Antigua and Barbuda, the Bahamas, Barbados, Belize, Grenada, Jamaica, Papua New Guinea, St. Christopher and Nevis, St. Lucia, St. Vincent and the Grenadines, the Solomon Islands, and Tuvalu.

Although the Queen is the Head of State, she has no direct role in passing legislation. The Queen formally approves legislation passed by Parliament. Not since the time of Queen Anne in 1707 has the monarch refused to give Royal Assent to a bill passed by Parliament. Parliament normally sits for five years unless dissolved earlier by the Queen. The Queen has the right to dissolve Parliament at any time and call for new elections in the House of Commons, but traditionally this has only been done at the request of her Prime Minister. The last time a monarch unilaterally dissolved Parliament was in 1834, during the reign of William IV.

The Queen regularly reads Cabinet and Foreign Office papers and has the right to be consulted. The Queen meets to confer on a weekly basis with her Prime Minister. Throughout England's long history many Prime Ministers and sovereigns have worked well together, while others have had less-than-cordial relationships.

She receives visiting Heads of State and pays official visits to overseas countries. Queen Elizabeth II is undoubtedly the most well-traveled Head of State in the world and has established relationships with the many

Queen Elizabeth II delivers the speech at the State Opening of Parliament in the House of Lords with the Duke of Edinburgh seated at her side.

current and former world leaders she has met during her long reign. The Queen's experience in working with past Prime Ministers, and her insights gleaned from her dealings with world leaders over the years, make her an invaluable resource for her Prime Minister as they confer each week to discuss affairs of state.

The Queen acts as the Head of the Commonwealth, composed of former territories of the British Empire. The Commonwealth was created at the end of WWII as a voluntary alliance of 54 independent countries to advance democracy, human rights, and economic and social development within the member countries. The Commonwealth's 1.7 billion people make up more than a quarter of the world's population. Member countries range in size from some of the world's largest and most populous countries, such as India, to some of its smallest, like Tuvalu, a group of small islands north of the Fiji Islands in the Pacific Ocean. During her reign, Elizabeth II has visited almost every member state and regularly meets with Commonwealth leaders.

The Queen carries out a number of important ceremonial functions as Head of State. She presides at the State Opening of Parliament. Typically, this occurs in November of each year, but may take place at other times, or even more than once a year if there is a change of government. The Queen holds formal garden parties each year at Buckingham Palace in London and Holyroodhouse in Edinburgh. The Queen bestows knighthoods and

The Queen Mother, Queen Elizabeth II, the Duke of Edinburgh, and the Prince of Wales on the balcony of Buckingham Palace after the 2001 Trooping the Color.

decorations at the investiture ceremonies held at Buckingham Palace, Holyroodhouse, and sometimes at Cardiff Castle in Wales. (See Honours and the Orders of Chivalry beginning on page 120.) She is the patron of countless charities and her year is filled with endless rounds of receptions and ceremonial functions.

Recently, there have been calls for reforming the monarchy and stripping it of many constitutional and financial powers, including removing the monarch's ceremonial involvement in governmental affairs and ending financial subsidies for the extended Royal Family. Under these proposals the monarch would no longer appoint the Prime Minister and give assent to laws. The report "The Future of the Monarchy," published in 2003 by the left-leaning think tank, the Fabian Society, has also proposed allowing non-Protestants to succeed to the throne; ending the Queen's role as Head of the Church of England; changing the Oath of Accession to allow the monarch to take early retirement; allowing succession to pass to the eldest child regardless of gender; and removing the right of the monarch to determine the spouse of those in line of succession, which could allow Prince Charles to marry his mistress, Camilla Parker-Bowles. Some argue that the monarchy is a useless anachronism in the 21st century and should be abolished, while others see value in a ceremonial Head of State who is not tied to any one political party or interest group, or beholden to any special constituency. To many the monarch serves as a much-needed symbol of tradition in this modern time of continuous change and is a unifying figure as Britain is transformed into a diverse, multi-cultural society. The debate on the future role of the monarchy will carry on as the monarchy continues to evolve.

The Queen's Wealth

Tabloid claims of the Queen's vast wealth have often been wildly exaggerated. They invariably include property held in trust by the Queen as sovereign on behalf of the nation, which is not her private property to do with as she pleases. The Queen sometimes refers to the Royal Family as the "firm," which is a good analogy. The Queen does not personally own the magnificent Royal Palaces, the Royal Art Collection, or the fabulous Crown Jewels any more than the President of the United States owns the White House, Air Force One, or the art in Washington D.C.'s National Gallery. In fact, according to *The Sunday London Times'* 2003 "Rich List," best-selling writer J.K. Rowling, author of the Harry Potter books, is richer than Queen Elizabeth II. *The London Times* reports that the richest man in Britain is the Duke of Westminster. His personal fortune, estimated at £4.9 billion, comes from property in central London, where he owns 300 acres of the most exclusive real estate in Mayfair and Belgravia.

The Queen has four sources of income. Parliament provides a fixed annual amount (called the "Civil List") to pay for the official expenses incurred by the Queen as Head of State. The Civil List is fixed at £7.9 million annually through 2011. Most of the money (about 70%) goes to pay for staff salaries and office expenses. The money from the Civil List also covers the costs of putting on official functions such as the Royal Garden Parties and State Visits.

In return for the Civil List, the monarch gives up the right to receive the hereditary revenues from the former Royal properties known as the "Crown Estate." After the Norman Conquest of 1066, all the land in the Kingdom "belonged" to the king. Down through the centuries, parcels of land were granted to nobles who supported the king or were sold to raise revenue for the crown. Finally, George III transferred the bulk of the remaining Crown Estate properties to Parliament at his accession in 1760, to be held in trust for the support of future monarchs in return for an annual stipend as set by Parliament.

The Crown Estate consists of substantial commercial and residential real estate holdings, including prime areas in central London—Regent Street,

Regent's Park Estate, St. James's, Kensington, Millbank, and Victoria Street—about 300,000 acres of agricultural land and forestry in England and Scotland, and extensive seashore and marine assets. A Board of Commissioners manages the Crown Estate, and the net income is paid to the government. Profits from the Crown Estate totaled £170.8 million for the year ending March 31, 2003, and the profits were received by the Exchequer for the benefit of the British people.

Royal Coat of Arms on Buckingham Palace gate.

The Queen also receives "Grants-in-Aid" from the government to maintain the Royal Palaces—Buckingham Palace, St. James's Palace, Clarence House, Kensington Palace, and Windsor Castle—and to pay for official travel expenses of the Queen and her entourage.

The other two sources of income for the Queen are the Privy Purse and her own personal income. The Privy Purse is funded from income received from the Duchy of Lancaster, which is a separate estate held in trust by the monarch since 1399. The Queen uses the income generated from the Duchy of Lancaster to support the other members of the Royal Family and to pay for their official expenses. The Duchy of Lancaster consists of 52,000 acres of primarily farmland. The Queen also earns private income from her personal investments, which are mostly held in blue chip stocks and bonds. The Queen and her husband, Prince Philip, are the only members of the Royal Family who currently receive funds from the Civil List. The Queen's finances are managed by the Keeper of the Privy Purse, who is part of the Royal Household.

Prince Charles, as the Prince of Wales, and his two sons, Prince William and Prince Harry, are supported from the Prince's independent income received from the Duchy of Cornwall, which is generated from real estate interests in Cornwall, Devon, Somerset, and south London. The Duchy of Cornwall has been the traditional source of income for the Prince of Wales since 1337, when King Edward III made his son the first Duke of Cornwall. The young princes also receive an independent income from the estate of their late mother, Princess Diana.

The Royal Palaces—Buckingham Palace, St. James's Palace, the Tower of London, Hampton Court, Clarence House, Kensington Palace, Windsor Castle, and the Palace of Holyroodhouse in Edinburgh, Scotland—the extensive Royal Art Collection, the Crown Jewels, and the Queen's State Jewelry are all held by the Queen as sovereign. They are a part of the national heritage maintained in trust by the monarch. The Queen privately owns Balmoral Estate in Scotland, which includes the castle and 50,000 acres of land. Balmoral Estate was purchased for Queen Victoria by Prince Albert in 1852. The Queen owns the elegant Sandringham Estate in Norfolk, which was built in 1870 by the Prince and Princess of Wales, who later ascended the throne as King Edward VII and Queen Alexandra. The Queen also has her own private collections of art, furniture, jewelry, and horses.

Since 1992, the Queen has consented to pay income tax and capital gains tax on her private income. Her net personal income and the net income from the Duchy of Lancaster received into the Privy Purse are fully taxable. The Civil List and the Grants-in-Aid are not considered income, but rather expense reimbursements for her duties as Head of State, and are not subject to income tax. Upon the Queen's death, the portion of the Queen's estate that will be passed on to her successor will not be subject to inheritance tax. The Queen's bequests to anyone other than the next sovereign will incur inheritance tax.

The Symbols of Royal Office

The sovereign's motto is *Dieu et mon Droit* ("God and my right"). It is sometimes attributed to Richard the Lion-Heart who supposedly said after being victorious in battle, "God and my right did this, not I." The motto of the sovereign appears below the shield on the Royal Coat of Arms. In the center of the Royal Coat of Arms is a shield displaying the royal emblems of the different parts of the United Kingdom: the three lions of England in the first and fourth quarters, the lion of Scotland in the second, and the harp of Ireland in the third. The shield is bordered by a garter displaying the motto of the Order of the Garter, *Honi soit qui mal y pense* (meaning "Evil be to him who thinks evil"). The shield is supported by the crowned English lion and Scottish unicorn and is topped by the royal crown. Below the shield is the motto of the sovereign. Sometimes above the motto you may see the plant emblems of the United Kingdom—the rose, thistle, and shamrock.

The Royal Standard is the flag bearing the Royal Coat of Arms that represents the Sovereign and United

The Queen's Royal Standard displayed on her car.

Kingdom. It is flown when the Queen is in residence in one of the Royal Palaces, on the Queen's car on official journeys, and on her aircraft when it is on the ground. It may also be flown on any building during official visits by the Queen. The Royal Standard is different from the familiar blue, white, and red Union Flag—the national flag of the United Kingdom. Popularly known as the "Union Jack," it symbolizes the union of England, Scotland, and Ireland. It bears the horizontal and perpendicular red cross on a white background (the symbol of St. George, patron saint of England), the diagonal white cross on a blue background (symbol of St. Andrew, patron saint of Scotland), and the diagonal red cross on a white background (symbol of St. Patrick, patron saint of Ireland). The Welsh emblem of a red dragon does not appear, as Wales is considered a principality of England. You may see the Union Jack flying over Buckingham Palace or Windsor Castle when the Queen is not in residence.

The Crown Jewels

The Crown Jewels are held in trust by the Queen as sovereign and can be seen in the Jewel House in the Tower of London. Most of the original Crown Jewels from the time of Edward the Confessor are gone—lost in 1266 when King John was fleeing from his rebellious barons over the tidal marshland of Wash in eastern England. The tide swept in and his baggage carrying the royal treasury was carried away by the incoming water. Some of the Crown Jewels were pawned during the English Civil War by Charles I's Queen. The remaining treasures were confiscated by Oliver Cromwell's men. The precious metal was melted down to pay the army and some of the jewels were sold. When Charles II was restored to the throne, the crown and Royal Regalia had to be remade for his coronation in 1661.

The Imperial State Crown is brought to the House of Lords for the State Opening of Parliament.

The largest and most imposing of the Crown Jewels is the Imperial Crown. It is worn at the coronation and for state occasions such as the State Opening of Parliament. It was made for the coronation of Queen Victoria in 1838 and has over 2,700 diamonds, pearls, and other precious stones, including a large ruby belonging to the Black Prince, which was worn by Henry V at the Battle of Agincourt. The Imperial Crown contains the huge 317-carat Second Star of Africa, cut from the Cullinan diamond found in South Africa. The crown is topped by the diamond-encrusted Maltese cross, which is set off by the large sapphire said to have been taken from the Coronation Ring found on the body of Edward the Confessor when his remains were moved in 1163 to the new tomb built for him by Henry III in Westminster Abbey.

At the Jewel House in the Tower of London, you will also see the beautiful St. Edward's Crown (fashioned from parts recovered from Edward the Confessor's original crown), the Golden Orb, the Scepter with the Cross, the Coronation Ring, and State Sword encrusted with diamonds, pearls and rubies. The Cullinan I—the largest cut diamond in the world—is set in the Sovereign's Scepter. The late Queen Mother's crown, made for her coronation in 1937 with George VI, contains the famed Koh-i-Noor diamond (meaning "mountain of light"), which came from India. The silver Anointing Spoon was made in 1399 for the coronation of Henry IV. Next to it is the 14th century, eagle-shaped vessel called an Ampulla. It holds the Holy Oils used for anointing the monarch during the coronation ceremony. The Anointing Spoon and Ampulla are the oldest pieces to have survived. They were hidden from Cromwell's men by monks at Westminster Abbey.

CHAPTER 4
A PRIMER ON ROYALTY, THE PEERAGE AND TITLES OF NOBILITY, HONOURS AND THE ORDERS OF CHIVALRY

Royalty

By tradition, in terms of precedence, the king ranks higher than his queen. The only time when an English king and queen have held the throne jointly as co-rulers was during the reign of William III and Mary II. The titles of prince and princess come from the Latin *princeps* (meaning "first in rank"). In 1917, King George V decreed that only the children of the monarch, the children of the sons of the monarch, and the eldest son of the eldest son of the Prince of Wales could receive the title of His or Her Royal Highness (HRH), Prince, or Princess. Queen Elizabeth II's children are all considered HRH, Prince or Princess, as are the sons of the Prince of Wales and children of the Duke of York. The children of the Queen's daughter, Anne, the Princess Royal, are not entitled to be called HRH, Prince, or Princess. The Queen's royal cousins, the Duke of Gloucester, the Duke of Kent, Princess Alexandra, and Prince Michael of Kent are entitled to their formal titles because of their status as grandchildren of King George V, but none of their children may claim the title.

A person may hold more than one noble title. In such a case, he is known by his highest title. For example, in 1947, shortly before his wedding to Princess Elizabeth (later Queen Elizabeth II), Lieutenant Philip Mountbatten was made Duke of Edinburgh, Earl of Merioneth, and Baron Greenwich. King George VI granted his new son-in-law the special style of "His Royal Highness." Despite all his additional titles, and status as the husband to the Queen, he is known as His Royal Highness (HRH) Prince Philip, Duke of Edinburgh.

Accession and Succession

You may have heard the phrase, "The King is dead. Long live the King." This is because the monarch succeeds to the throne immediately upon the death of the prior sovereign so there is no break in the continuity of succession to the throne, even though the ceremonial coronation may take place much later. After an Accession Council is held in St. James's Palace, which is attended by members of the Privy Council, the Lord Mayor of London, and government leaders, the new monarch is publicly proclaimed from the balcony overlooking St. James's Friary Court. Then proclamations are read out at various sites across the realm. Succession is no longer purely a matter of hereditary right, but is determined through the Act of Settlement passed by Parliament in 1701 to ensure that no Catholic would succeed to the throne. All monarchs rule by consent of Parliament. The new monarch is required to be in "communion with the Church of England," as the sovereign acts as Head of the Church of England. Marriage to a Catholic removes the monarch's heir from the line of succession.

By custom, male heirs take precedence over daughters in order of their birth. A daughter of the monarch takes precedence over the sovereign's brothers and may become Queen Regnant, ruling in her own right, as opposed to Queen Consort—reigning by virtue of her marriage to the king. There have only been seven British queens who have ruled as Queen Regnant: Queen Mary I (the daughter of King Henry VIII); Queen Elizabeth I (the second daughter of King Henry VIII); Mary, Queen of Scots (Queen of Scotland only); Queen Mary II (daughter of James II and joint ruler with King William III); Queen Anne (second daughter of James II); Queen Victoria; and Queen Elizabeth II.

Queen Elizabeth II's mother, the former Lady Elizabeth Bowes-Lyon, married Prince Albert, Duke of York, who was second in the line to the throne. He later became King George VI when his brother, King Edward VIII, abdicated in 1936. His wife, Elizabeth, became Queen Consort. Upon the death of her husband, George VI, in 1952, the Queen did not like the term Queen Dowager normally used by the King's widow. She chose instead to be called "Her Majesty Queen Elizabeth, the Queen Mother," although she was popularly known as the "Queen Mum."

If a monarch dies without any surviving children, the crown passes to the eldest brother of the sovereign and then to his brother's children in order of birth. This was the case when George IV died and was succeeded by his brother William IV (George III's third son). William IV died without leaving any legitimate children (although he had ten illegitimate children with his longtime mistress) and so the throne passed to Queen Victoria, who was the daughter of Edward, the late Duke of Kent, George III's fourth son. Only when the monarch has no surviving brothers or descendants of brothers does the crown pass to the sovereign's sisters, who take precedence by age, as was the case with Queen Anne.

The heir apparent is the person next in line to the throne. It is usually the eldest son of the sovereign, but it could be the eldest grandson, as was the case with George III who succeeded his grandfather, George II. Prince Charles is heir apparent to Queen Elizabeth II. The

Investiture of the Prince of Wales at Caernarvon Castle, by his mother, Queen Elizabeth II.

heir apparent to the throne has been ceremonially granted the title of Prince of Wales. In 1301, Edward I formally created the title "Prince of Wales" for his son. The title is not automatic, but rather is ceremonially conferred on the designated heir apparent by the monarch. The motto of the Prince of Wales is *Ich Dien* (meaning "I serve"). It appears on his crest, which has three feathers rising through a gold coronet of alternate crosses and *fleur-de-lys*. The motto *Ich Dien* dates from the time of Edward, the Black Prince, and the Battle of Crécy in 1348.

The Queen granted Prince Charles the title of Prince of Wales in 1958, when he was 9 years old. Prince Charles was ceremonially invested as Prince of Wales in 1969, when he turned 21. If Prince Charles dies, then his eldest son William would become the heir apparent, because no other birth could supercede his place in the line of succession.

The Coronation

The coronation is an elaborate religious ceremony which dates back over a thousand years to the coronation of the Saxon King Edgar, at Bath, in 973. The ritual officially crowning the monarch was largely devised by Archbishop Dunstan (later St. Dunstan). Since the year 1066, every coronation of an English monarch has been held at Westminster Abbey. The service is derived from Old Testament accounts of the anointing of Saul and David by Samuel. Queen Elizabeth II ascended to the throne upon the death of her father, George VI, on February 6, 1952, but her coronation did not occur until June 2, 1953, as the ceremony took many months to plan.

In the coronation ceremony, the monarch is formally recognized and accepted by the people, and then takes the oath promising to govern according to law, exercise justice with mercy, and uphold the Church of England. Seated in the chair made for King Edward I's coronation in the 13th century, the monarch is anointed, blessed, and consecrated by the Archbishop of Canterbury. The monarch is then invested with the symbols of royalty—the Orb and Scepter, and the Crown of St. Edward. Finally, the new monarch receives the homage of his or her subjects as the assembled churchmen and nobles pledge their allegiance to the Crown.

Peerage and Titles of Nobility

A "peer" is a person who holds a title of nobility conferred by the sovereign. After the Norman invasion, the term "nobility" was originally applied to all ranks above commoners and included earls, barons, knights, and esquires. With the establishment of the House of Lords, a distinction came to be made between hereditary nobility (the Hereditary Peerage) and the lower ranks of nobility. Knights, esquires, and gentlemen were no longer considered peers, as their titles were not inherited.

The five British titles of peerage ranked in order of seniority are duke, marquess, earl, viscount, and baron. The title of duke comes from the Latin *Dux* (meaning "leader"). First created by King Edward III in 1337, the duke is the highest hereditary rank below that of a prince. The wife of a duke is called a duchess. The Queen's husband, Prince Philip, is Duke of Edinburgh. The Queen's second son, Prince Andrew, is Duke of York. Prince George, Duke of Kent, and Prince Richard, Duke of Gloucester, are the Queen's first cousins. For his wartime service to the nation, Winston Churchill was offered, but declined, the Dukedom of Dover.

The title of marquess is the English equivalent of the French *marquis* and ranks between a duke and an earl. Following the Norman invasion, it was the title given to the nobles who guarded and defended the King's interests in the Welsh or Scottish "marches" or border territories. The wife of a marquess is a marchioness.

The third-ranking title is the earl, which comes from the Norse *jarl*. It is the oldest English title and reflects the many years of Viking invasions and England's rule by the Danes during the 10th century. It is equivalent to the French title of count. The earl or count is the principal noble of the county. The wife of an earl is a countess. The oldest earldom is the earldom of Arundel, which dates back to 1433. Prince Edward, the third son of Queen

Elizabeth II, was created the Earl of Wessex and Viscount Severn upon his marriage. The title of viscount comes from the French *vice-comes*, meaning the count's deputy. It ranks between an earl and a baron. The wife of a viscount is a viscountess.

Queen Elizabeth's coronation June 2, 1953.

Originally, barons were nobles who were given their lands directly from the monarch as a reward for service to the crown. The term comes from the Latin *per baroniam* (meaning "directly"). The majority of titled nobility in Britain today are barons. The wife of a baron is called a baroness.

The title of baronet (not to be confused with the peerage title of baron) is a form of hereditary knighthood. It is an honor conferred by the Crown and is inherited within a family. However, baronets are not considered peers and are not entitled to a seat in the House of Lords. James I invented the title of baronet in order to raise money for his Irish wars.

Peers can be either Life Peers or Hereditary Peers. Hereditary Peerages are inherited by the peer's eldest son, or, if there is no surviving son, then the title passes to his closest male heir. The other children of a peer are considered commoners, but may have a "courtesy title" based on their parent's rank. The title of a peer can become extinct if there is no male heir to take it, although some peerages may be passed on to a daughter. The last Hereditary Peerage was granted by Queen Elizabeth II in 1964.

As the term suggests, the titles of Life Peers, unlike Hereditary Peers, cannot be passed on to their heirs. Life Peerages have been used by monarchs for centuries to reward favorites or recognize subjects who have rendered outstanding service to "King and Country." Charles II granted Life Peerages to many of his mistresses. In modern times, Life Peerages have been created by the monarch to honor distinguished persons who have rendered exceptional service to the country. They are given the titles of baron or baroness. Former Prime Minster Margaret Thatcher was granted a Life

Peerage as Baroness of Kestevan. In addition, her husband, Denis Thatcher, was made a baronet, which allowed their son, Mark Thatcher, to inherit his title. Since enactment of the Life Peerages Act of 1958 by the MacMillan Conservative Government, the ranks of Life Peers have expanded to include women, who are allowed to sit and vote in the House of Lords for their life-time only. The Prime Minister usually nominates candidates for a Life Peerage, or the Leader of the Opposition or other party leaders may propose a candidate, but peerage is bestowed by the Queen.

Being a Peer is not what it used to be. Prime Minister Tony Blair's Labour government was elected in 1997 with a platform of reforming the House of Lords and turning the house into a more representational legisla-tive body. While Hereditary Peers can still pass their titles to their heirs, the House of Lords Act of 1999 removed the right of most of the Hereditary Peers to sit and vote in the House of Lords.

Honours and the Orders of Chivalry

Originally, the honor of knighthood was related to military service. Today, the honor of knighthood is used to recognize extraordinary service to the Crown or exceptional contributions in the advancement of British arts, literature, or science. There are about 22 investitures held every year. The investiture ceremonies are usually held at Buckingham Palace, the Palace of Holyroodhouse in Edinburgh, Scotland, and occasionally at Cardiff Castle, Wales, on St. David's Day (the patron saint of Wales). Investitures are nor-mally performed by the Queen, but the Prince of Wales may also carry out Investitures on behalf of the Queen. The lists of names of those to be hon-ored are published each year for the Queen's Birthday Honours (announced on the Queen's official birthday in June) and for the New Year Honours.

British subjects receiving the honorary knighthood (except clergy) receive the traditional dubbing of the sword on each shoulder by the Queen (called an "accolade"). Foreigners who receive honorary knighthoods, such as Rudy Giuliani, the former Mayor of New York City, are presented to the Queen to receive their honor, but they are not dubbed. Ordinary knights are known as Knight Bachelors. After their elevation to knighthood, British sub-jects are entitled to be addressed as "Sir" or "Dame," such as rock star, Sir Elton John, or actress, Dame Judi Dench.

There are several Orders of Chivalry used by the monarch to confer special honor. The Order of the Garter, the Order of the Thistle, the Order of

Merit, and the Royal Victorian Order are Chivalrous Knighthoods granted to recipients who are chosen exclusively at the discretion of the Queen. Other honors are conferred by the sovereign upon the advice of the Prime Minister. Knighted members of the various Orders of Chivalry are entitled to place special initials after their names signifying the class of the order they have received. For example, in the Order of the Bath, the initials GCB (Grand Cross, Bath), KCB or DCB (Knight or Dame Commander, Bath), and CB (Companion, Bath) are used, depending on their rank in the order.

The Order of the Garter is the oldest and the highest honor the sovereign can bestow. The Order of the Garter dates back to April 23, 1348. According to legend, Edward III was dancing with the beautiful Countess of Salisbury when her garter slipped from her leg onto the floor. The King knelt and gallantly replaced her garter and told onlookers, *"Honi soit qui mal y pense"* (meaning "Evil be to him who thinks evil"). Historians suggest the garter emblem developed from a military strap worn by English knights during the French campaigns carried out under Edward.

The Knights of the Garter wear blue velvet robes, plumed hats, and the gold and blue Garter insignia on their left breasts. The order is limited to 25 members. Foreign monarchs may be admitted as Stranger Knights. Appointments to the order are announced on April 23—St. George's Day. The new Knights of the Order of the Garter are inducted by the sovereign in an elaborate ceremony held in St. George's Chapel at Windsor Castle, during which a gold and blue garter is attached to the Knight's left leg. The grand ceremony is held on the first Monday of Royal Ascot week in June of each year.

The Order of the Thistle is sometimes referred to as the Scottish equivalent of the Order of the Garter. It represents the highest honor in Scotland. Its origins are shrouded in Scottish legend, but the order was revived by Queen Anne in 1703. In 2000, the Queen's daughter, Princess Anne, was honored with the Order of the Thistle in recognition of her work with the Save the Children Fund and over 200 other charitable organizations.

The Most Honorable Order of the Bath was established by King George I in 1725 to reward conspicuous service to the Crown. It is the second-highest order of chivalrous knighthood in England. It is primarily awarded to officers serving in the armed forces, but there is a civil division as well. The Order takes its name from the knight's ritual of the bath taken prior to the formal ceremony of knighthood. The Knights of Order of the

Bath are inducted by the Sovereign in a ceremony held in the Henry VII Chapel at Westminster Abbey.

Insignia of the Order of the Garter on display at Windsor Castle.

The Orders of the British Empire were created by George V during the First World War in 1917. The sovereign bestows three levels of Orders of the British Empire. The highest is Commander of the British Empire (CBE). The second is Order of the British Empire (OBE). The third is Member of the British Empire (MBE). Their motto is "For God and the Empire." Members are inducted in the chapel in the crypt of St. Paul's cathedral, and a ceremony is held once every four years to celebrate the Orders.

The Order of Merit was established by Edward VII in 1902. The Order is limited to 24 living British subjects. Current members include the Queen's husband, His Royal Highness, the Duke of Edinburgh; the Queen's son, His Royal Highness, the Prince of Wales; former Prime Minster Margaret Thatcher (now Baroness Thatcher); opera legend Joan Sutherland; painter Lucian Freud; and playwright Thomas Stoppard. Past honorees have included Prime Minister Sir Winston Churchill and Florence Nightingale. Orders of Merit have also been awarded to a handful of foreigners, including Dr. Albert Schweitzer; former U.S. General Dwight D. Eisenhower; former South African President Nelson Mandela; and the late Mother Teresa.

The other Orders of Chivalry which may be bestowed by the sovereign include the Most Distinguished Order of St. Michael and St. George; the Order of St. Patrick; the Royal Victorian Order; the Royal Victorian Chain; the Order of the Companions of Honor; the Most Venerable Order of St. John of Jerusalem; the Order of the Star of India; and the Order of the Indian Empire.

CHAPTER 5
PLANNING YOUR TRIP—EXPERIENCING ROYAL LONDON

There are any number of events during the year where you can enjoy the full pomp and pageantry of Royal London during your visit. Before you leave home, you can check for the most current information on the London Travel Links provided on the publisher's Web site, www.europeincontext.com. You might want to check on the British and London Tourist Authority official Web sites, www.visitbritain.com/uk, and www.londontouristboard.com, or try England's or London's Web sites, www.visitengland.com, and www.londontown.com. Information about royal events may also be found on the official British Monarchy Web site, www.royal.gov.uk and www.royalinsight.gov.uk.

When you arrive in London, check in the local paper to see if there any Royal Galas or official visits scheduled during your stay. You might check out the "Court Circular" published in *The London Times* to see what the Royals are up to during your visit. When planning your trip, remember that the opening and closing times often vary with the season and change with little notice. Many of the sites discussed in this book may be closed for state occasions. Be sure to confirm the opening and closing times when you arrive.

You may wish to stop by the main Britain and London Visitor Centre. It is located at No. 1 Regent Street, which is between Trafalgar Square and Piccadilly Circus. It is open on Monday 9:30 a.m. - 6:30 p.m., Tuesday - Friday 9:00 a.m. - 6:30 p.m., and Saturday - Sunday 10:00 a.m. - 4:00 p.m. The Centre offers information desks for England, Wales, Scotland, and Ireland and provides a full range of travel services, including help with travel arrangements, accommodations, and theater and event reservations. Look for your free copies of the *London Planner* published each month by VisitBritain, the *Time Out Guide* published by Time Out Guides and the British Tourist Authority, or *The London Guide* published by Transport for London. These free monthly guides offer helpful, up-to-date information about what is going on during your stay.

Westminster Bridge and Big Ben.

123

◆ Changing the Guard (Mounting the Guard)

The surest way to get a taste of Royal London is to attend the famous Changing of the Guard. The Queen's London residence at Buckingham Palace is protected day and night by Her Majesty's Guards. Sentries are also posted at St. James's Palace, the Tower of London, and Windsor Castle. The ceremonial handing over of the duty of Queen's Guard from one regiment to another takes place daily at 11:30 a.m. from March until August and on alternate days from September until February—depending on the unpredictable London weather. There is no guard ceremony in wet weather. The main action takes place behind the gates inside the forecourt of Buckingham Palace.

The ceremony actually begins at 11:00 a.m. when the St. James detachment of the old guard assembles for inspection in Friary Court at nearby St. James's Palace. The guard then marches down the Mall to join the Buckingham detachment, which has assembled in the forecourt of the palace. At 11:30 a.m. the new guard arrives from the Wellington Barracks on Birdcage Walk and marches into the forecourt of the palace to relieve the old guard. The captains of the guard exchange the keys to the palace—symbolically passing on the responsibility of safeguarding the monarch to the new guard. At precisely 12:05 p.m. the old guard exits through the center gate and returns down Spur Road to Birdcage Walk to Wellington Barracks.

The Changing of the Guard provides London's most colorful daily royal display with the guards marching in their bright red tunics and tall bearskin hats (called "busbies") accompanied by a military band, which plays

throughout the 45-minute ceremony. The band plays a variety of music, from traditional military marches to show tunes. The huge crowds that assemble to watch the spectacle make it difficult to see anything, but if you get there early enough you can try to find a good spot with a view on the steps of the Victoria Monument, or you can stake out a place near the central gates of the palace to watch the action up close.

There is also a smaller changing of the mounted members of the Life Guards and Blues and Royals who mount the

The Guard exiting the forecourt of Buckingham Palace.

Queen's Life Guard protecting the Horse Guards Parade—the former official entrance to Buckingham and St. James's Palaces. The mounting of the Life Guards and Blues and Royals occurs daily at Horse Guards Arch off Whitehall at 11:00 a.m. (Sunday 10:00 a.m.). The Regimental Guards on duty at Windsor Castle and the Tower of London also have a ceremonial Changing of the Guard.

The Household Division is made up of two regiments of Household Cavalry—the Life Guards and the Blues and Royals—and five regiments of the Foot Guards—the Grenadiers, the Coldstream Guards, the Scots Guards, the Welsh

(above and below) The Household Division Band accompanies the Changing of the Guard.

Guards, and the Irish Guards. The members of the Household Division are all drawn from the active military and are fully trained, operational troops, who have fought with distinction in every conflict in which Britain has been engaged, including peacekeeping efforts in Bosnia and during the recent Iraq War. After you have seen the Changing of the Guard, you might want to continue your pursuit of Royal London by visiting the nearby Queen's Gallery and the Royal Mews.

♦ The Queen's Gallery

Around the corner from Buckingham Palace is the Queen's Gallery. It is the only part of Buckingham Palace that is open to the public year round. It contains exhibitions of art and other treasures from the Royal Collection. The original building was designed by John Nash as a conservatory overlooking the gardens, but was converted into a private chapel for Queen Victoria in 1843. A German bomb destroyed the chapel on

September 13, 1940. It was redeveloped as a gallery for the Royal Collection in 1962. The gallery was recently renovated and reopened by the Queen in 2002. The rotating exhibitions include displays of paintings, prints, drawings, watercolors, furniture, porcelain, miniatures, enamels, jewelry, and other works of art. Entry is by timed ticket. If you have not purchased advance tickets, you should try to come by as soon as it opens, as tickets do sell out in the summer. To get there from the front of

The Queen's Gallery.

Buckingham Palace (if you are facing the palace), walk to your left and bear right, which leads to Buckingham Palace Road. The Queen's Gallery will be down on your right.

Opening hours

Open daily 10:00 a.m. - 5:30 p.m. (last admission 4:30 p.m.). Entry is by timed ticket. (Closed April 18, December 25-26.)

To purchase tickets

On-line

Go to www.the-royal-collection.com/royaltickets

Group tickets E-mail: groupbookings@royalcollection.org.uk.

By telephone

Credit card sales (0) 20 7766 7301/ Fax: (0) 20 7930 9625

In person

Tickets may be purchased from the ticket desk at the Queen's Gallery, subject to availability.

♦ The Royal Mews

Just past the Queen's Gallery further down on Buckingham Palace Road, you will find the Royal Mews or stables, where you can see the fabulous horse-drawn carriages used for Royal and State Occasions, State Visits, Royal Weddings, and the State Opening of Parliament. The Royal Mews were reconstructed in 1825 by John Nash for George IV to house the royal horses and carriages and to store the magnificent ceremonial harnesses and livery.

In the Carriage House you can see the amazing Golden State Coach used for coronations. It was designed in 1761 for George III and has been used in every coronation since George IV. The Golden State Coach weighs

4 tons, is 24 feet long, stands 12 feet high, and takes 8 horses to pull. The coach is gilded in 22-karat gold and has panels painted by Giovanni Cipriani.

The Golden State Coach on display.

The Irish State Coach was made for Queen Victoria in Dublin in 1852 and is still used by the Queen for the State Opening of Parliament. The open-topped landau was used in 1981 in the wedding of Charles and Diana—the Prince and Princess of Wales— and then again in 1986 for the wedding of Andrew and Fergie—the Duke and Duchess of York. The Glass State Coach was made in 1910 and carries new ambassadors when they are officially presented to the Queen. The Royal Mews also serves as the royal garage, housing the three-ton Phantom Six Rolls Royce presented to Queen Elizabeth II for her Silver Jubilee.

Opening hours
October – July: Open daily 11:00 a.m. - 4:00 p.m. (last admission 3:15 p.m.).
August - September: Open daily 10:00 a.m. - 5:00 p.m. (last admission 4:15 p.m.).

To purchase tickets
On-line
Go to www.the-royal-collection.com/royaltickets.
Group tickets E-mail: groupbookings@royalcollection.org.uk.

By telephone
Credit card sales: (0) 20 7766 7302/ Fax: (0) 20 7930 9625

In person
Tickets can be purchased at the Ticket Office in the Royal Mews Shop.

♦ Ceremony of the Keys
Another easy way for you to connect with London's royal past is to attend the Ceremony of the Keys at the Tower of London. This ancient ceremony has been performed at the Tower in one form or another every night for the last 700 years, as the gates of the Tower are safely locked under guard and the keys delivered to the Resident Governor of the Tower. Tickets to the ceremony are available to the public free of charge, but you must apply in writing at least two months in advance (for June - August). Send a self-addressed envelope, state the names of the people in your party (up to

127

seven per request), and provide an International Reply Coupon. You may purchase the coupon at your local Post Office. The size of each evening's group is limited and so in the summer, you may wish to specify more than one alternate day when you would be able to attend. Your admission pass will be mailed to you.

Sunset over the Tower Bridge seen from the Tower.

Visitors with their admission passes are admitted to the Tower of London at 9:30 p.m. Be there on time as late arrivals are not admitted! The Yeoman guide, wearing his long red coat and black Tudor bonnet, explains the history and significance of the ceremony to the assembled group and then leads them inside the Tower down to Traitors' Gate, where they can observe the ceremony. The Chief Warder emerges from the Byward Tower carrying a candle lantern and the Queen's Keys. He comes to Traitors' Gate to meet his military escort. He hands the lantern to one of the guards. The escort and Chief Warder then proceed to lock the outer gates. All guards and sentries salute the Queen's Keys as they pass. After locking the outer gates, the Chief Warder and his escort return to Traitors' Gate, where they are challenged by a sentry.

The group then proceeds through the Bloody Tower archway and up towards the steps leading to the Tower. At the top of the stairs the main escort stands waiting at attention. The escort presents arms in salute as the Chief Warder raises his Tudor bonnet in the air and calls out, "God preserve Queen Elizabeth!" The assembled guard responds, "Amen." The clock chimes ten and the bugler sounds Last Post. The Chief Warder then hands over the keys to the Resident Governor and the guard is dismissed. The ceremony is concluded precisely at 10:05 p.m., after which the visitors are conducted to the exit. The combination of the nighttime setting at the Tower illuminated by floodlights, the small group, and the knowledge that you are witnessing a 700-year-old tradition endows the brief, solemn ceremony with a magical sense of royal history that makes this truly worthwhile.

To order tickets, write to:
The Ceremony of the Keys
Waterloo Block
HM Tower of London
London EC3N 4AB, UK

♦ Westminster Abbey

Westminster Abbey holds a unique place in Britain's history and tradition, and no tour of Royal London would be complete without a visit to the venerable abbey. It was not included as one of the twelve audio tours because visitors may use the excellent audio guides, which are available for a small fee, or they may take one of the many the guided tours offered during the day. According to legend this is the site of the church built by Sebert, King of the East Saxons. It was consecrated by Mellitus, first Bishop of London in 616. However, the earliest written records show that a Benedictine abbey, dedicated to St. Peter, was here in 730. The area where the church was erected was originally on a small island in the Thames known as the Isle of Thorns.

Construction of the present church was begun by Edward the Confessor in 1050. The church was consecrated on December 28, 1065. The good King died the following week and was buried here. On December 25, 1066, William the Conqueror was crowned here. Thus Westminster Abbey was established as the official site for coronations and funerals for the crown. Every English monarch except Edward V (one of the "Little Princes in the Tower") and Edward VIII (who abdicated to marry Wallis Simpson) was crowned here. It is also the burial place of eighteen monarchs. The last sovereign to be buried in the abbey was George II, who died in 1760.

Westminster Abbey is obviously a prime tourist destination, and the jostling hordes of tourists can detract from your experience of this world-class treasure. If at all possible, try to time your visit to Westminster Abbey for later in the day when the throngs of tourists have lessened, or come back on Wednesday evening, when the

The Gothic north façade of Westminster Abbey.

129

abbey reopens from 6:00 p.m. to 7:00 p.m. You can pick up the audio guide from the information desk located to the right as you enter, or you can check there for the starting time of the next guided tour.

Visitors are directed in a clockwise route around the abbey's interior. After your visit to the tombs and monuments in the sanctuary, you may visit the Cloisters, the Chapter House, the Crypt, and Pyx Chamber. The Chapter House is called the cradle of representative and constitutional government because the King's Great Council first met here in 1257 under Henry III. It later became the House of Commons, which continued to meet here until the deliberations were moved across the street to the Chapel of St. Stephens in Westminster Palace in 1547.

Opening hours

Monday - Friday Open 9:30 a.m. – 4:45 p.m. (last admission: 3:45 p.m.); Wednesday the abbey is open for a second session 6:00 p.m. – 7:00 p.m.; Saturday 9:30 a.m. – 2:45 p.m. (last admission 1:45 p.m.). Sunday the abbey is open to worshipers only. Check out its Web site, www.westminster-abbey.org. Guided tours are given for an additional charge. The 90-minute tours include the Shrine of Edward the Confessor, the Royal Tombs, Poets' Corner, the Cloisters, and the Nave. Audiotape guides may be rented for an additional charge at the Information Desk located by the North Entrance. The Audiotape guides are available Monday - Friday 9:30 a.m. – 3:00 p.m.; Saturday 9:30 a.m. - 1:00 p.m. Note that there are no public restrooms in Westminster Abbey or the Cloisters.

To purchase tickets

Tickets can be purchased on the day of your visit at the ticket desk located to the right as you enter through the north entrance near St. Margaret's Church.

Getting there

By Underground

Westminster Abbey is best reached by the Westminster Tube station, which is served by the Jubilee, District and Circle Lines. Use Exit #5. You will see the abbey on the other side of Parliament Square. Turn right onto Great George Street, then take the first crosswalk you come to. Cross Great George Street and go past Parliament Square. Cross Broad Sanctuary to the North entrance of the abbey beside the entrance to St. Margaret's Church.

♦ State Opening of Parliament

The Queen formally opens the new session of Parliament each year, usually in October or November. The Queen rides from Buckingham Palace to Westminster Palace in the Irish State Coach, escorted by members of the Household Cavalry and

Queen Elizabeth II and Prince Philip at the 1999 State Opening of Parliament.

accompanied by military bands. When the procession reaches the Houses of Parliament, the Queen enters through the Royal Entrance and goes into the Royal Robing Room, where she puts on her crown and ceremonial robes.

The Queen then processes through the Royal Gallery and takes her place on the throne in the House of Lords, where the Lords have gathered in attendance in their Parliamentary robes. The Gentleman Usher of the Black Rod (most often referred to simply as "Black Rod") is sent to the House of Commons to summon the Members (the "MPs"). When Black Rod arrives, the door is ritualistically slammed in his face. Black Rod knocks three times on the door before he is allowed in. The ritual symbolizes the right of the House of Commons to debate without interference from the House of Lords. The Prime Minister and Leader of the Opposition then lead all the MP's into the House of Lords. The Lord Chancellor hands a speech to the Queen who reads it out to the assembled Lords and MPs. The speech is written by the Prime Minister's office and contains the new government's agenda for the new session. Before the State Opening ceremony begins, the cellars of the Palace of Westminster are searched by the Yeomen of the Guard—a ritual dating back to the Gunpowder Plot of November 1605, when Guy Fawkes and his co-conspirators tried to blow up Parliament and kill King James I.

You cannot attend the actual proceedings in the House of Lords, but you can find a spot to enjoy the colorful Royal Procession as the Queen, escorted by regiments of the Household Division, travels to and from the Houses of Parliament.

♦ Visiting the Houses of Parliament

Visiting the Houses of Parliament is easy for British residents who can make the arrangements through their MP. Overseas visitors can take guided tours of the Houses of Parliament only during the several weeks when Parliament is not in session during the late summer and

St. Stephen's Entrance by Westminster Hall.

early fall. Check the Parliament Web site, www.parliament.uk/ visiting, to confirm the dates when guided tours are available. This is generally during the periods of July - August and September - October.

Opening hours

Open Monday, Tuesday, Friday, and Saturday 9:15 a.m. - 4:30 p.m.; Wednesday and Thursday 1:15 p.m. - 4:30 p.m.

To purchase tickets

On-line

Go to www.firstcalltickets.com.

By telephone

Credit card sales (0) 20 870 906 3773

The 75-minute "Line of Route Tour" starts at the Sovereign's Entrance, and includes the Queen's Robing Room, the Royal Gallery, the Prince's Chamber, the House of Lords Chamber, the Peers' Lobby and Corridor, the Central Lobby, Commons Corridor and "No" Lobby, the House of Commons Chamber, St. Stephen's Hall, Westminster Hall, and New Palace Yard. The tours offer a chance to see the spectacular interiors of the former Palace of Westminster.

When Parliament is in session during the year, anyone can usually visit the Strangers' Galleries in the House of Commons or the House of Lords and can listen in on the afternoon and early evening debates. When the flag is flying over the Victoria Tower, it means the House of Lords is in session. When House of Commons is in session, the light atop the Big Ben is illuminated.

You can check on the Parliament Web site to see if Parliament will be sitting during your stay or just look for the long lines if you are passing by

The Household Guards march in formation past the Queen and Royal Family in the annual Trooping the Color.

Parliament Square. The best time to go is after 6:00 p.m. when the crowds have died down. The line for the House of Lords is generally shorter. The lines for each house form outside St. Stephen's Entrance beside Westminster Hall and Old Palace Yard. The debates are generally boring, but it offers a wonderful opportunity to see the interiors.

♦ Trooping the Color

Perhaps the most colorful annual royal event is the spectacular ceremony of Trooping the Color, where the regiments of the Household Division—the traditional guardians of the Royal Family—and their Massed Bands perform in a martial pageant at the Horse Guards Parade in early June in honor of the Sovereign's Official Birthday. The Queen's actual birthday is April 21st. Trooping the Color, also known as The Queen's Birthday Parade, involves over 1,400 soldiers, 200 cavalrymen on horseback, and 400 band members, including bagpipe and drum units. It is an experience you will never forget!

The ceremony dates back to the early days of warfare when the regimental flag was the rallying point for troops in battle. The parade of flags or colors was used to teach each soldier to recognize his own regimental color. The custom of honoring the Sovereign's Birthday with this military parade began in 1748 for George III, but was temporarily suspended during the

Prince Philip takes the salute in the Colonel's Review.

period of the King's mental illness. The ceremony was restored on the accession of his son, King George IV, and became—with the exceptions of the two World Wars and a cancellation in 1955 caused by a national rail strike—an annual event.

The soldiers of the Foot Guards, the Household Cavalry, and the Massed Bands assemble at the Horse Guards Parade, where they are joined by members of the King's Troop Royal Artillery, the ceremonial artillerymen with their horse-drawn gun battery. Members of the Royal Family arrive by carriage and enter the Horse Guards Building to watch the parade from the large window over the central arch leading to Whitehall. The Queen and Prince Philip, Duke of Edinburgh, are escorted by a Sovereign's Escort of the Household Cavalry in a grand procession down the Mall from Buckingham Palace to the Horse Guards Parade. The Queen is greeted by a Royal salute and then carries out an inspection of the assembled troops.

The Massed Bands perform as they execute elaborate marching drills across the parade ground. The "Color" or Regimental Flag is then trooped down the lines of assembled Guards. Only one regiment's color is trooped each year. The Guards then march past the Queen in a series of quick and slow marches accompanied by the Massed Bands. The Mounted Troops and the Royal Horse Artillery walk and trot past the Queen in salute.

When the march-pasts have been completed, the Queen returns with her mounted escort to Buckingham Palace at approximately 12:15 p.m., where there is a ceremony in the forecourt of the palace and the Changing of the Guard continues. The King's Troop Royal Horse Artillery fires an artillery salute in nearby Green Park at approximately 12:52 p.m. At 1:00 p.m., the Queen and members of the Royal Family gather on the balcony of Buckingham Palace to witness a fly-by salute by the Royal Air Force

Members of the Household Band march across Horse Guards Parade in the 2003 Trooping the Color.

(weather permitting).

There are actually three opportunities to witness the event first-hand. There are two dress rehearsals on the two Saturdays before the actual event, which is typically held the second Saturday in June. The first rehearsal is called "The Major General's Review." The Major General commanding the Household Division takes the salute. The next Saturday there is "The Colonel's Review." It is usually attended by Queen Elizabeth II's husband, Prince Philip, Duke of Edinburgh. The final Trooping the Color is attended by the Queen and the entire Royal Family and is quite an event.

Competition is understandably fierce for seats in the bandstands that are erected around the perimeter of the Horse Guards Parade, and so seats are allocated by a lottery. It is easier to get tickets for the two rehearsals. You will need to apply in writing to the Headquarters Household Division between January 1 and March 1 for the tickets for that year's event. Send a self-addressed envelope with an International Reply Coupon. State the names of the people in your party, the date of your arrival in Britain, and where you plan to be staying. Successful applicants will be notified in writing and advised of the cost of their tickets. Seats for the first rehearsal (The Major General's Review) are free. Successful applicants must confirm their acceptance in writing and send payment within 21 days after notification. Your payment must be made by International Money Order or bank check in British pounds. You can obtain these from your local bank. Check out the Household Division Web site, www.army.mod.uk/ceremonialandheritage /events.

To order tickets, write to:
The Brigade Major Headquarters Household Division Horse Guards, Whitehall
London SW1A 2AX, UK

The Queen's mounted Life Guards.

Even if you are not successful in obtaining tickets to the seated area, it is still worth- while to plan your visit to coincide with this fantastic event. You can join the throngs of people who gather to watch the Royal Procession as the cavalry and troops escort the Queen along the Mall to and from Buckingham Palace and the Horse Guards Parade. The procession departs from Buckingham Palace around 10:30 a.m. and returns at approximately 12:15 p.m.

♦ Beating Retreat
Beating Retreat is another annual musical spectacle of sound and color, performed by the Massed Bands of the Household Division on two succes- sive evenings in June at Horse Guards Parade. Beating Retreat has its origins in the past when the beating of drums, the parading of the guards, and the ceremonial lowering of flags at the end of the day signaled the closing of camp gates for the night.

The band members are drawn from the bands of the two Household Cavalry Regiments and the five Foot Guards Regiments of the Household Division. The Massed Bands march up Birdcage Walk from Wellington Barracks to the Horse Guards Parade for the two performances. The event starts at 7:00 p.m. each evening with the Queen or other members of the Royal Family usu- ally in attendance. The exact dates vary each year. Be sure check one of the British or London tourist Web sites before you leave to confirm the date.

♦ Remembrance Sunday
The annual ceremony held at 11:00 a.m. on the Sunday closest to November 11—the date and time when World War I ended—was initially intended to honor the fallen of WWI. It was expanded to honor those lost

in WWII and, in 1980, the remembrance ceremony was widened once again to honor "all who have suffered and died in conflicts in the service of their country and all those who mourn them." The tolling of Big Ben and a gun salute mark the start of the two minutes of silence that begin at 11:00 a.m. The silence ends with the bugler from the Household Division playing Last Post before the Queen lays a wreath of red poppies at the base of the Cenotaph on behalf of the whole nation. Senior members of the Royal Family, the Prime Minister, other politicians, and representatives of religious communities also lay wreaths of poppies at the solemn stone monument designed by Edwin Lutyens. Finally, there is a military march down Whitehall past the Cenotaph down to Parliament Square, along Great George Street, down Horse Guards Road and back to the Horse Guards Parade. Huge crowds gather to watch the somber ceremony. It is essential to be in place well in advance. The event is televised and is also shown on large outdoor screens set up at various points nearby.

♦ Royal Gun Salutes

As part of the Household Troops, the duties of the King's Troop Royal Horse Artillery include the firing of Royal Salutes in Hyde Park on Royal Anniversaries and State Occasions, and providing a gun carriage and teams of black horses for state and military funerals. Gun Salutes are given at Hyde Park on February 6 (the anniversary of the Queen's accession); April 21 (the Queen's actual birthday); June 2 (the anniversary of the Queen's coronation); June 11 (Prince Philip, Duke of Edinburgh's, birthday); and on State Occasions such as the State Opening of Parliament or State Visits. If one of the anniversary dates falls on a Sunday, then the salute is given the following day. Gun salutes are also given by the Honourable Artillery Company, which was formed by King Henry VIII in 1537 and is based at the Tower of London. It fires a 62-gun salute at 1:00 p.m. on these same days.

The King's Troop Royal Horse Artillery.

CHAPTER 6
THE ROYAL PALACES AND FORTRESSES

Some of the current and former Royal Palaces and Fortresses in or near London are open for visitors. Buckingham Palace—the official London residence of Queen Elizabeth II—is open to the public for only six weeks in late summer. However, the Tower of London, nearby Windsor Castle, Hampton Court, Kensington Palace, and Greenwich Palace are regularly open and allow you excellent opportunities to catch a glimpse of the royal lifestyle for yourself.

♦ Buckingham Palace

Buckingham Palace is the symbol of Royal London. When the Queen's standard is flying over the palace, you know the Queen is in residence. Buckingham Palace is where the Queen receives and entertains important guests on State Visits, and where many ceremonial and official occasions, State Banquets, and Investitures are held.

History of Buckingham Palace

Buckingham House was built in 1702 for John Sheffield, the First Duke of Buckingham. George III acquired the property in 1762 for his private residence so that his young bride, Queen Charlotte, could have a quiet place to retreat from the rigid formality of court at nearby St. James's Palace. When George IV came to the throne, he directed his architect, John Nash, to remake the palace into a theatrical showplace, worthy of being the official center of his resplendent court. Parliament authorized only £200,000 for the ambitious project. Nash quickly went over budget trying to comply with the King's extravagant demands. Nash's design called for a three-sided court open on the eastern side facing St. James's Park. He built the Marble Arch as a grand ceremonial entranceway to the palace to commemorate the English victories at Trafalgar and Waterloo, but, after it was completed, it was discovered that the Royal State Coaches were too wide to fit through the gate! The Marble Arch was moved to Hyde Park in 1851.

When George IV died, the renovation was still not completed. The King's frugal 64-year-old brother, William IV, preferred the less grand Clarence House located beside St. James's Palace. When the cost overruns exceeded £700,000, Nash was finally dismissed from the project. Architect Edward Blore was chosen to finish the palace along the lines of Nash's designs. Shortly after her accession in 1837, Queen Victoria moved from Kensington Palace into the unfinished Buckingham Palace. Victoria soon found that the small residential suite in the new palace could not accommodate the needs of her growing family. Thomas Cubitt added a fourth wing designed by Edward

The proud façade of Buckingham Palace.

Blore. It enclosed the eastern side of the palace, which now faces the Mall and creates a quadrangle in the center. After Prince Albert's death, the Queen retired to Windsor Castle and made few appearances at the palace.

When Victoria's son, Edward VII, finally came to the throne in 1901, he completely remodeled the interior. In 1913, during the reign of his son, George V, the entire façade was replaced in Portland stone according to the design of Sir Aston Webb, who had also redesigned the grand approach down the Mall to the Queen Victoria Memorial. The forecourt of the palace (where the Changing of the Guard takes place) was completed in 1911 as part of Webb's Victoria Memorial scheme.

Planning Your Visit

The State Rooms of Buckingham Palace are open to the public for six weeks from mid-August until September when the Royal Family is away vacationing in Balmoral Castle, Scotland. Visitors purchase their timed entry ticket, which allows a certain number of visitors to take the prescribed route through the palace every 15 minutes throughout the day. At the time indicated on the time-stamped ticket, visitors enter through the Ambassadors' Court located to the south (on the left if you are facing the front of the palace). Visitors then exit though the gardens to a temporary souvenir shop set up by the exit.

Opening hours

August 1 – September 28 *exact dates may vary:
Open daily 9:30 a.m. - 4:30 p.m. (last admission 4:15)

To purchase tickets

On-line

Go to www.the-royal-collection.com/royaltickets.

Group tickets E-mail: groupbookings@royalcollection.org.uk.

By telephone

Credit card sales: (0) 20 7766 7300/ Group credit card sales: (0) 20 7766 7321

In person

Tickets may be purchased at the Ticket Office at Canada Gate in Green Park, subject to availability. It is strongly recommended that you purchase your tickets in advance.

Getting there

By Underground

Buckingham Palace is located at the western end of St. James's Park and can best be reached by Underground at either the Green Park or Victoria Tube station. The easiest walk is from Green Park Tube station, which serves the Piccadilly, Victoria, and Jubile Lines. Exit the Green Park tube station using the "Piccadilly South" exit. Turn right through the gate into Green Park and follow the path downhill to reach the palace in a leisurely 5-minute walk. From the Victoria Tube station, which serves the Circle, District, or Victoria Lines, exit onto Buckingham Palace Road and turn right. Cross over to the other side of the busy street. The 15-minute walk will take you past the Royal Mews and the Queen's Gallery near the visitors' entrance.

By bus

Buckingham Palace may be reached on bus routes 7, 11, 211, 139, C1, and C10, which stop on Buckingham Palace Road.

♦ Tower of London

The Tower of London is steeped in English royal history and should not be missed! It is open year round and, with the amazing Crown Jewels on display, it is an essential stop on your visit to London.

History of the Tower

Shortly after he was crowned on Christmas Day 1066, William I began building this fortress by the Thames on the site where Claudius, the Roman Emperor, had built defensive fortifications more than a thousand years earlier. Traces of the Roman wall can still be seen within the Tower grounds and just outside the exit from the nearby Tower Tube station. William's temporary wooden stronghold was soon replaced by one built of cream-colored stone brought over from France. The White Tower was completed by William the Conqueror's sons, William II and Henry I. Inside were a banqueting hall, the small St. John's Chapel, council chambers, and rooms for the Royal Family and their servants and soldiers, as well as a prison and dungeon.

Tower of London viewed from the Thames.

The White Tower stood 90 feet high and had 15-foot-thick walls. The tower was entered by a single door placed 15 feet from the ground level so that the stairs could be withdrawn in case of attack. Today, a wooden staircase will take you inside the second floor entrance to the White Tower. (The lower windows were added by Christopher Wren in the 1660s.) The interior stairwell was constructed with stairs ascending counter-clockwise so that defenders could more easily fight off attackers trying to force their way up the stairs. Three wells provided an ample water supply for the Tower during any siege.

Henry II added kitchens and a bakery. During the reign of Henry II's son, Richard I the Lion-Heart, his Chancellor, William Longchamp, Bishop of Ely, was left in charge of the Tower. Richard's brother John attempted to take the throne in the King's absence. John besieged the Tower and forced Longchamp to surrender.

John's son, Henry III, built interior walls, dug the moat, erected a watergate to provide a fortified river entrance, and whitewashed the Conqueror's original Tower, giving rise to its nickname—the "White Tower." He also began a royal menagerie, which included an elephant sent by the French King Louis IX in 1255. Henry III's son, Edward I, built the Byward Tower and Traitors' Gate, completed the inner and outer walls, and added the Royal Mint.

Henry VIII added the half-timbered house looking out onto Tower Green, known as the Queen's House. It was built for his second wife, Queen Anne Boleyn. The Tower was used as a prison for the many who fell from Henry VIII's favor, including Sir Thomas More, Bishop Fisher, and Thomas Cromwell, as well as his wives, Anne Boleyn and Catherine Howard, who were both executed on Tower Green.

Lady Jane Grey's nine-day reign ended when she was beheaded on Tower Green in 1554. Queen Mary's half-sister, Princess Elizabeth, was imprisoned in the Tower for three months while she was questioned about her knowledge of anti-Catholic plots against Mary. During the English Civil War, the Parliamentary forces captured and held the Tower when Charles I retreated to Oxford. The Tower was renovated during the reign of Queen Victoria and was opened to the public. By the time of Queen Victoria's death in 1901, over a half million people were visiting the Tower each year.

The White Tower.

The Tower suffered no damage during WWI, but eleven German spies were held and later executed at the Tower. The Tower suffered bomb damage from several air raids in WWII. Rudolf Hess, Hitler's Deputy Minister, was held in the Queen's House for four days in May of 1941. The last execution at the Tower was that of the German spy Joseph Jakobs, carried out on August 14, 1941.

Planning Your Visit

The Tower of London is one of the most popular stops on any visit to London, and so it is generally very crowded. Typically, there are long lines at the ticket windows to get into the Tower grounds. Once inside there are more long lines to enter the White Tower and Jewel House—the top attractions at the Tower. It is best to buy your admission ticket in advance and come early to get to the Tower when it first opens. You may purchase tickets from any London Tube station, and go directly to the Tower entrance.

Once inside you should go directly to the Jewel House and save the famous Yeoman Warder tours or exploration of the other Tower sights until after you have seen the dazzling Crown Jewels. You will not be disappointed. Once inside the Jewel House, the lines will take you through rooms with screens continuously playing video footage of Queen Elizabeth II's coronation in 1953 and pictures of the Royal Regalia. The line will then take you past a number of displays of silver and gold plate, robes, and scepters before leading you to the main room, where a moving sidewalk will glide you past

The Jewel House, where the Crown Jewels are kept under watchful eye.

either side of the display case with the Crown Jewels. You may circle back around to get on the moving sidewalk to see the jewels again if you like, or you may move up onto the platform viewing area above the display case, where the Jewel House Wardens stand watch over the Royal Regalia. Feel free to ask the guards any question you might have, but photographs of the Crown Jewels are not allowed.

After you have seen the Crown Jewels, you might then want to visit the White Tower. Inside the Tower you can explore four floors of exhibits about medieval life, various instruments of torture, models of the Tower, and displays from the Royal Armor collection, including three sets of armor for King Henry VIII. On the second floor is the tiny Chapel of St. John the Evangelist, where the Royal Family and the court worshipped and where the knights of the Order of the Bath hold their vigil the night before a coronation.

Your visit to the Tower should include a Yeoman Warder Tour to hear their vivid retelling of the fascinating stories of the Tower. The free, hour-long guided tours are led by the Yeoman Warders about every thirty minutes throughout the day. Henry VIII formed the Yeoman Warders of the Tower in the 16th century. According to one tale, the nickname "Beefeaters" dates from 1669, when Cosimo de Medici, the Grand Duke of Tuscany, visited London. He was amazed at the Yeoman Warders' capacity for consuming vast quantities of beef, and his comment has stuck in the popular imagination. There are about forty Yeoman Warders, drawn from former warrant officers of Her Majesty's Armed Forces who have at least 22 years of distinguished service. Their formal uniform is the bright red tunic embroidered with the Queen's monogram, EIIR, and large, white, ruffled collar. Yeoman Warders are usually seen at the Tower in the blue undress uniform granted to them by Queen Victoria in 1858. About 150 people still live within the Tower grounds, mainly the Yeoman Warders and their families.

If you have the time, there is still so much more to see in the Tower grounds. Audio guides may be rented just inside the Tower entrance. The audio narration covers areas not included in the Yeoman Warder Tour. The Bloody Tower is furnished with period furniture as it might have appeared during the thirteen years Sir Walter Raleigh was imprisoned there for displeasing James I. You may visit Beauchamp Tower, named for Thomas Beauchamp, Earl of Warwick, who was imprisoned here by Richard II from 1397 to 1399. On the walls of Beauchamp Tower, you can still read graffiti scratched in stone by the miserable prisoners held there before their executions.

A plaque marks the spot at Tower Green where seven prisoners were executed, including Anne Boleyn and Catherine Howard (two of the six wives of Henry VIII), Lady Jane Grey (the nine-day Queen), and Robert Devereux, Earl of Essex (Elizabeth I's impetuous former favorite). The interior of the Chapel of St. Peter ad Vincula is accessible only as part of the Yeoman Warder Tour. However, you can also attend Sunday morning services, which take place in the Chapel every Sunday, except during the month of August. Services begin at 11:00 a.m. If you want to attend a service in the Chapel, you should enter the Tower grounds through the West Gate along the Thames side past the Traitors' Gate.

You may visit the prison cell in the Bell Tower where Sir Thomas More was supposedly held for the last fourteen months of his life before he was beheaded. You can walk around the inner wall of the Tower and enjoy the views of the Tower Bridge over the Thames. Although the Tower Bridge looks very old, it was built in 1894. Look for the signs directing you to the Martin Tower, where you can begin the wall walk, which ends at the Salt Tower. Parts of the Medieval Palace, which include St. Thomas's Tower, the Wakefield Tower, and the Lanthorn Tower, are open to the public. Here you can enjoy reconstructed interiors showing daily life during the reign of Edward I in the 13th century.

You will see ravens boldly strutting the grounds. According to legend, Charles II was told that if the ravens left the Tower, the kingdom would fall, and so he ordered that ravens be kept here permanently. Their wings are clipped to prevent escape and they strut around the Tower Green. You can visit their cages, which you will find next to the Wakefield Tower. Be careful! The ravens are definitely not tame and may peck at you if you get too close.

Opening hours

November 1 - February 28: Open Tuesday – Saturday 9:00 a.m. - 5:00 p.m.; Sunday - Monday 10:00 a.m. - 5:00 p.m. (last admission 4:00 p.m.) (closed

December 24–26, January 1).

March 1 – October 31: Open Monday – Saturday 9:00 a.m. - 6:00 p.m.; Sunday 10:00 a.m. - 6:00 p.m. (last admission 5:00 p.m.).

To purchase tickets

On-line

Go to www.hrp.org.uk.

By telephone

Credit card sales: (0) 870 756 7070

In person

Tickets can be purchased on the day of your visit at the Tower of London ticket offices, but you would be advised to buy your ticket in advance from any London Tube station and avoid the long ticket line. Tickets may be purchased up to seven days in advance. You might want to buy a Combination Ticket allowing entry to the Tower of London, Hampton Court Palace, and Kensington Palace. The Combination Tickets can be purchased at their respective ticket offices.

Getting There

By London Underground

The Tower can be reached on the Circle and District Lines. Exit at the Tower Hill Tube station and follow the signs leading to the main entrance of the Tower.

By Docklands Light Railway (DLR)

The Tower can be reached on the Docklands Light Railway. Exit at the Tower Gateway Station, which is located next to Tower Hill Tube station, and follow the signs leading to the main entrance of the Tower.

By bus

The Tower can be reached on the city bus routes 15, 25, 42, 78, 100 and D1 or by the major sightseeing bus tours.

By riverboat

The Tower can be reached by riverboat from Charing Cross, Westminster, or Greenwich piers. Disembark at the Tower Pier located directly in front of the Tower.

♦ Windsor Castle

Windsor Castle is the Queen's favorite residence and has served as a Royal Palace and fortress for over 900 years. It is the largest and oldest occupied castle in the world today. Located only twenty miles west of London, Windsor Castle is a perfect day trip away from the big city of London. The castle is set in the scenic town of Windsor along the banks of the River

View of the Round Tower from the Thames.

Thames, with the venerated Eton College located across the river.

History of Windsor Castle

William the Conqueror selected this strategic site alongside the River Thames for one of the series of fortresses he was building to keep his rebellious Saxon subjects in check. Windsor Castle was only a day's march from the Tower of London and it guarded the western approaches to the city. The castle, built on a chalk bluff rising a hundred feet above the Thames, provided control over river traffic into the interior.

The earth and wood fortifications erected by William the Conqueror were rebuilt in stone by his son, Henry I. The improvements were continued by Henry II, who added the Round Tower and the surrounding stone curtain walls of the Upper Ward. The fortifications were sorely tested in 1194, when Henry's son, John, rebelled against his brother, Richard I, while the King was away on crusade in the Holy Land. Nobles loyal to Richard besieged Windsor Castle but failed to take it. In 1215, English nobles confronted King John in a meadow at Runnymede not far from Windsor Castle, where he was forced to recognize their rights in the *Magna Carta*. Windsor was besieged again by angry barons the following year, when John reneged on his pledge.

John's grandson, Edward I, spent much of his childhood at Windsor. It was here in 1254 that young Edward married his future queen, Eleanor. Their grandson, Edward III, was fascinated by the legendary tales of King Arthur and the Knights of the Round Table. He founded the Order of the Knights of the Garter and sought to remake the castle to reflect the medieval ideals of Christian chivalry. Edward erected the inner gatehouse and towers, established the College of St. George, and built new royal apartments, the Great Hall, and the Royal Chapel—spiritual home to the Knights of the Garter.

In 1475, Edward IV began building St. George's Chapel beside Henry III's old chapel. The new chapel's original wooden roof was replaced by intricate fan vaulting built in stone during the reign of Henry VII. It was completed in 1528 during the reign Henry VIII, who also added the imposing entrance gate to the Lower Ward that bears his name.

Parliamentary forces seized Windsor Castle during the English Civil War. After his trial and execution, Charles I was laid to rest in St. George's Chapel. Windsor resumed its role as a Royal Residence under Charles II. Charles's architect, Hugh May, created the fabulous State Apartments, which are adorned with ornate woodcarvings by Grinling Gibbons and Henry Phillips, and beautiful ceiling paintings by Antonio Verrio.

George III and George IV were responsible for the final major improvements to the castle that we see today. George III moved to Windsor Castle in 1789, after he recovered from his first bout with the crippling disease porphyria. His son, George IV, took up residence at Windsor Castle in 1828; had his architect, Jeffrey Wyattville, raise the Round Tower an additional thirty feet to its current 215-foot height; added extra towers and battlements to give the castle a more theatrical look; and rebuilt the vast St. George's Hall.

Windsor Castle reached its peak as the center of court life during the reign of Queen Victoria, who lived at Windsor for most of the year. She entertained much of European royalty here, including Tsar Nicholas I and Napoleon III. Her beloved Albert died unexpectedly of typhoid in 1861 while the Royal Family was in residence at Windsor. Queen Victoria converted the old Henry III chapel beside St. George's Chapel into the Albert Memorial Chapel. Albert's mausoleum was erected at nearby Frogmore Estate.

The Royal Family's identity was so tied to the castle that in 1917 George V proclaimed the family name of Saxe-Coburg-Gotha (from Queen Victoria's husband, Prince Albert) would henceforth be the House of Windsor.

During the Second World War, the future Queen Elizabeth II and her sister, Princess Margaret, were sent to the comparative safety of Windsor Castle while their parents braved the worst of the Blitz. Queen Elizabeth II considers the castle as her primary residence and regularly spends her private weekends here, as well as official Court residences at Easter and during Ascot Race Week in June. The Queen's standard flies above the castle when she is in residence.

On November 22, 1992—the 45th wedding anniversary of the Queen and Prince Philip—a fire broke out. An electrical workman's spotlight ignited the curtains by the altar in Queen Victoria's private chapel. Over 100 rooms in the castle were damaged or destroyed by the fire. Fortunately, most treasures and works of art had been

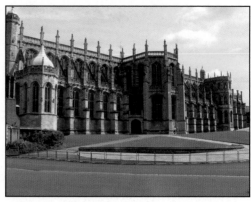

St. George's Chapel.

removed temporarily. It took 250 firefighters over fifteen agonizing hours to put out the blazing fire. The huge cost of renovating the castle led Queen Elizabeth II to open Buckingham Palace to the public for the first time in its history. Windsor Castle was reopened in 1997 after five years of extensive renovation, in time to celebrate the 50th wedding anniversary of the Queen and Prince Philip.

Planning Your Visit

The castle itself covers over thirteen acres. Because Windsor is a working Royal Residence, much of the castle is not open to the public and the grounds may be closed for State ceremonial functions. After you buy your admission ticket you should rent the excellent audio guide. It will give you a first-rate description of all there is to see at Windsor. There is surprisingly little signage inside the castle and grounds. The grounds of Windsor Castle are divided into three sections—the Upper, Middle, and Lower Wards. Once you go through the Admissions Centre, you will walk up though St. George's Gate, where you will come to an exhibition describing the history of the castle. However, if you arrive when the castle first opens, you might want to hurry past the exhibition to get ahead of the surge of visitors and come back later to enjoy this introductory exhibit. In the Lower Ward you will find the exquisite Chapel of St. George and the Albert Memorial Chapel. In the Middle Ward is the Round Tower, which is not open to visitors. In the Upper Ward you will find the North Terrace leading to the State Apartments with Queen Mary's Dolls' House and the Gallery of Drawings. At certain times of the year, the Semi-State Apartments are also on view.

As a Royal Residence, Windsor Castle has its own Changing of the

Guard, which takes place at 11:00 a.m. Monday through Saturday from April to June. From July to March, the ceremony takes place on alternate days. If your visit to the castle is on a day when the Changing of the Guards is occurring and you arrive before 11:00 a.m., you should first go down to the Lower Ward to explore St. George's Chapel so that you will time your visit to be in a good position to view the Changing of the Guard. The ceremony is performed just below the Chapel on the paved section to the right of the gate and the Lower Ward Gift Shop. You can also see part of the ceremony outside the Henry VIII Gate at 10:50 a.m. and 11:25 a.m. as the guards enter and exit the castle grounds.

If you arrive after 11:00 a.m. or on a day when the Changing of the Guard is not being performed, you should first walk past the imposing Round Tower with its deep moat (now a delightful garden) to the Upper Ward to explore the State Apartments and then finish your visit in the Lower Ward. The exit from the castle grounds is through the Henry VIII Gate. If you plan to return to the castle later in the day, you can get a return ticket from any of the gift shops.

The North Terrace offers lovely views over the Thames valley to Eton. Before you enter the State Apartments, take a few moments to visit the Drawings Gallery, which displays rotating exhibitions of treasures from the Royal Library. Another popular attraction is Queen Mary's Dolls' House. The diminutive mansion was built in 1924 by Sir Edwin Lutyens, who designed

London's Cenotaph. Queen Mary's Dolls' House is built on a scale of 1 to 12 and has two working elevators, running water and electricity, diminutive furniture, and even tiny books and paintings.

The self-guided route takes you through the State Apartments to the 180-foot long St. George's Hall—the dazzling setting for the Queen's largest State Banquets. The rooms are furnished with incredible treasures from the Royal Collection including masterworks by Cannaletto, Holbein, Rubens, Leonardo da Vinci, Rembrandt, Van Dyck, and English

Gardens at Windsor Castle.

painters such as Hogarth, Gainsborough, and Reynolds, as well as fine tapestries, porcelain, sculpture, and armor. From September to March, visitors can also enjoy George IV's lavish private apartments known as the Semi-State Rooms. At other times of the year, these splendid rooms are used by the Queen for official functions.

The Windsor State Apartments.

After you exit the State Apartments, return down the hill to the Lower Ward to see the exquisite St. George's Chapel— one of the finest examples of Gothic architecture in England. St. George's Chapel is used by the Royal Family when in residence and is the site for many royal christenings, confirmations, weddings, and funerals. St. George's Chapel was the site of the wedding in 1999 of Queen Elizabeth II's third son, Prince Edward, to Sophie Rhys-Jones. The chapel is the resting place of ten sovereigns and many members of the Royal Family: Edward IV, Henry VI, Henry VIII with his third wife, Jane Seymour, Charles I, George III, George IV, William IV, Edward VII and his wife, Alexandra, George V and his wife, Mary, and George VI and his wife, Lady Elizabeth Bowes-Lyon—the Queen Mum. The ashes of Queen Elizabeth II's sister, Princess Margaret, were placed beside her parents' tomb.

The chapel is dedicated to St. George, the patron saint of the Order of the Garter. Banners of the Garter Knights can be seen above the richly carved wooden stalls in the choir. During a grand ceremony, held on the Monday of Royal Ascot week in June, thousands of specially invited guests gather to observe the procession of the Queen and the Knights and Ladies of the Order of the Garter from the Upper Ward into the chapel.

Opening times and access may be restricted at certain times of the year, when official functions are scheduled. Check to confirm if the castle will be open during your visit. Even if the State Apartments are closed, the castle grounds and St. George's Chapel are worth the trip. St. George's Chapel is closed to tourists on Sundays, but worshippers are welcome. The public is welcome to attend Evensong service in St. George's Chapel, held at 5:15 p.m. daily.

It is a delight to simply stroll around Windsor Castle, and to explore the charming town of Windsor, which is nestled between the castle and the Thames. You can enjoy the surrounding countryside with a boat excursion on the Thames. As you exit from the Henry VIII Gate, continue straight onto Church Street. Most of the houses date from the 17th century. Look for the Burford House, where it is said Charles II kept his favorite mistress, Nell Gwynne, close at hand. The Parish Church and the Guildhall, built by Sir Christopher Wren, who was the architect of St. Paul's Cathedral, are both worth a quick stop. The Windsor Information Centre is located at 24 High Street, just past Victoria's statue, and directly across from Wren's Guildhall. Check out the Windsor tourism Web site, www.windsor.gov.uk.

Eton College, founded in 1440 by Henry VI, is located just across the river from Windsor. Walk downhill on High Street away from the castle. Cross the Windsor Bridge and continue on past enchanting antique stores and shops until you reach Eton College. The college has a Museum of Eton Life that is worth a quick look. Eton is a boys-only boarding school for privileged lads between the ages of 13 and 18. Its former pupils include nineteen British Prime Ministers. Princes William and Harry are both recent graduates of Eton. Check out the Eton Web site, www.etoncollege.com.

Opening hours

March – October: Open daily 9:45 a.m. - 5:15 p.m. (last admission 4:00 p.m.). November – February: Open daily 9:45 a.m. - 4:15 p.m.
(last admission 3:00 p.m.). *dates may vary due to official court functions. (Windsor Castle is closed Garter Day—the first Monday in Royal Ascot week in mid-June, Easter, December 25-26. The State Apartments are closed during Royal Ascot week in mid-June. The Semi-State Rooms are generally open late September through late March. St. George's Chapel is open Monday - Saturday, but is closed Royal Ascot week in mid-June, December 23, when the Chapel closes at 1:00 p.m., and December 24-26).

To purchase tickets

On-line

Go to www.the-royal-collection.com/royaltickets.

By telephone

Credit card sales: (0) 20 7766 7304

In person

Tickets can be purchased on the day of your visit from the Admissions Centre on Castle Hill opposite the Henry VIII Gate.

Getting there

By train

You can get to Windsor easily by two different routes, departing from either Paddington or the Waterloo train stations. The train from Waterloo is direct and the train from Paddington has one simple change of trains.

Paddington Train

The Thames Train offers service from Paddington Station to Windsor with a change of trains at Slough. When the train reaches Slough (after about 35 minutes), you should disembark, go up the stairs, turn left, and cross over the elevated walkway to Platform 1, where you can catch the train to Windsor. The train from Slough will take you the short remaining distance to Windsor (about 10 minutes) arriving at Windsor's Central Station. Check the full timetable for the Thames Train service from London Paddington to Windsor via Slough on www.thamestrains.co.uk. As you exit the station, you will enter a shopping arcade. The signs will indicate the way out to the street. High Street will be to your right, and Thames Street extends downhill to your left. The outer walls of Windsor Castle will be directly in front of you. Turn right onto High Street and go the short block to the intersection of Castle Hill and High Streets. You will see the bronze statue of Queen Victoria in the intersection. The Admissions Centre is further up Castle Hill, on the right.

Waterloo Train

South West Trains operates a direct service to Windsor and Eton's Riverside Station. The trip takes about 55 minutes. Check the full timetable for the South West Train service from London Waterloo to Windsor on www.swtrains.co.uk. When you reach Windsor you will disembark at the Riverside Station. Exit through the doorway on your left onto Datchet Road and turn right. Go one short block down Datchet to the intersection and turn left up Thames Street. You will see a monument to George V on the left. Walk up Thames Street until you come to the Queen Victoria statue at the intersection of Thames Street and Castle Hill. Turn left up Castle Hill.

By bus

The Green Line operates daily services from Victoria Coach Station, London. Check on its Web site, www.greenline.co.uk. Various tour companies operate a daily service to Windsor Castle, with pickup from many London hotels. For details, ask at your hotel.

By car

Follow the signs from all the major local roads. From the M4 take Exit 6, or from the M3 take Exit 3, and follow the signs to the paid parking lots in the town.

♦ Hampton Court

Hampton Court is located only twelve miles southwest of London. The quick trip is within

The Great Clock at Hampton Court.

travel Zone 6. You can explore 500 years of royal history during your visit to Hampton Court and its 60 acres of historic gardens along the River Thames.

History of Hampton Court

Hampton Court was originally the grand country house of Thomas Wolsey, who was made Henry VIII's Lord Chancellor in 1515. The previous year, Wolsey obtained the lease on the land from the Knights Hospitallers of St. John of Jerusalem, a religious order founded in the early 12th century. In 1525, Wolsey offered the estate to Henry in the vain hope of staying in favor. Within months of taking over Wolsey's home, Henry began a gigantic rebuilding project that lasted ten years. Henry built huge kitchens and an enormous Great Hall to serve his many guests and retainers. He also built the Chapel Royal with a magnificently carved and gilded wooden ceiling. For six days in August of 1546, Henry VIII used Hampton Court to extravagantly entertain the French ambassador's party of 200, plus 1,300 members of his own court.

Henry's third wife, Jane Seymour, died here while giving birth to Henry's long-awaited son and heir, Edward VI. Henry married wife number six, Catherine Parr, here in the Chapel Royal. His daughter Mary spent her honeymoon at Hampton Court with her husband, Phillip II of Spain. Hampton Court was often used for Royal entertainments during the reigns of Elizabeth I and her successors, James I and Charles I.

At the end of the English Civil War, Charles I was held at Hampton Court as a prisoner. After three months, he escaped, but was recaptured, tried for treason, and executed in 1660. Oliver Cromwell became Lord

Protector and later took over Hampton Court as his country home. In the Restoration, Charles II frequently used Hampton Court for entertaining.

During the reign of William III and Mary II, William preferred the healthy country air of Hampton Court. He stayed there while Kensington Palace was being built as his London residence and then divided his time between the two palaces. William and Mary engaged the great architect Christopher Wren to renovate Hampton Court. Wren planned to demolish the old-fashioned Tudor palace entirely and rebuild it in the new style. Luckily, Wren could only afford to rebuild the King and Queen's main apartments. In 1702, William died from complications after his horse stumbled on a molehill while the King was out hunting near Hampton Court.

Hampton Court Palace was last used as a Royal Residence during the reign of George II. The Queen's State and Private Apartments were redecorated and refurnished for George's wife, Queen Caroline, by William Kent, but the palace fell into disuse as a Royal Residence after 1737. The palace suffered no harm during the two world wars, but on March 31, 1986, a major fire swept through the King's Apartments causing severe damage. Luckily, only one painting and a few pieces of period furniture were damaged. The palace has an interesting exhibit on the renovation efforts carried out after the fire.

Planning Your Visit

After you purchase your ticket at the building located to the left as you enter the main gates, continue on to the Information Centre located in the Clock Court, where you can pick up the audio guide (included with your admission ticket). Unless you are traveling with small children, don't waste your time with the overrated guided tours, which are conducted at various times during the day by the rather tired costumed guides. Use the audio guide instead. First visit Henry VIII's State Apartments, which offer a fascinating glimpse into life at the Tudor court. The route through the State Apartments includes the Great Hall with its exquisite hammer-beam roof and magnificent tapestries and the Gallery, said to be haunted by the ghost of Henry VIII's fifth wife, Catherine Howard, who was arrested here and charged with adultery. The tour of the State Apartments ends at the beautiful Chapel Royal. Next return to the Clock Court and follow the signs to the starting point for the tour through the mammoth Tudor Kitchens. The kitchens display the scene as if the palace cooks were in the process of preparing food for the feast of St. John the Baptist, Midsummer's Day in 1542.

If you have the time, the magnificent King's State Apartments of William III and the Queen's State Apartments, built for his wife, Queen Mary, are well worth seeing for the impressive work of Sir Christopher Wren. Be sure to save time to visit the Wolsey Rooms, which are thought to have been part of Cardinal Wolsey's original private residence. The Wolsey Rooms lead to one of the best collections of Renaissance paintings in England, including works by Cranach, Bruegel, Correggio, Bronzino, Parmigianino, and Titian. You can also see Andrea Mantegna's *Triumphs of Caesar*, a series of nine paintings, on display in the Lower Orangery. The Georgian Rooms with the dull private apartments of George II and his Queen Caroline are less inspiring and can be missed.

Use any remaining time you have to enjoy the extensive 60 acres of Hampton Court Gardens with its Privy and Knot Gardens and its famous Maze. Near the Lower Orangery is the "Great Vine." It is reputed to be the oldest grape vine in the world still producing grapes. The 120-foot Great Vine was planted in 1768 by Lancelot "Capability" Brown, the famous 18th-century English landscape gardener who led the development of the naturalistic "English" style of gardening. There is a café and restaurant in the Tiltyard Gardens.

Opening hours
March 30 – October 25: Open Monday 10:15 a.m. - 6:00 p.m.; Tuesday - Sunday 9:30 a.m. - 6:00 p.m. (last admission 5:15 p.m.).
(closed December 24-26, January 1).
October 26 – March 29: Open Monday 10:15 a.m. - 6:30 p.m.; Tuesday - Sunday; 9:30 a.m. - 4:30 p.m. (last admission 3:45 p.m.).
The Hampton Court gardens are open all year round from 7:00 a.m. to dusk.

To purchase tickets

On-line
Go to www.hrp.org.uk.

By telephone
Credit card sales: (0) 870 753 7777

In person
Tickets can be purchased on the day of your visit at the ticket desk located on the left side of the driveway, just past the main entrance gate. Combination Tickets allowing entry to Hampton Court, Tower of London, and Kensington Palace can be purchased at their respective ticket offices.

Getting There

By train

South West Trains offers direct service departing from London's Waterloo Station to Hampton Court at 26 and 56 minutes past each hour. The train trip takes 32 minutes. When you arrive at Hampton Court, exit the train station and turn right. Cross the bridge and turn right into the main gates. Hampton Court is an easy 2-minute walk from the station. Note: Hampton Court is in travel Zone 6.

By bus

Hampton Court may be reached on bus routes 111, 216, 411, 416, 451, 461, 513, 726 and R68.

By car

Hampton Court is located on the A308. Follow the signs from all the major local roads. From the M25 take either exit 10 onto the A307 or exit 12 onto the A308.

By riverboat

Riverboats run in the summer from Westminster Pier to Hampton Court. The journey from Westminster can take up to 4 hours depending on the tides.

♦ Kensington Palace

Kensington Palace is best remembered as the London home of the late Diana, Princess of Wales—the place where thousands of flowers were left at the ornate gated entrance in tribute to the "People's Princess." Kensington Palace was also the childhood home of the future Queen Victoria and remains the residence of several other members of the extended Royal Family today.

History of Kensington Palace

When William III and Mary II came to the throne in 1688, Whitehall Palace was the principal Royal Residence in London. William III suffered from asthma, and hated the damp palace. In 1689, the King purchased the "country house" from the Earl of Nottingham and commissioned Christopher Wren and Nicholas Hawksmoor to convert it into his London Royal Residence. Wren constructed separate Royal Apartments for the King and Queen, a council chamber, a Chapel

Detail of the front gate at Kensington Palace.

156

Royal, and a 96-foot-long Gallery. The Royal Apartments were built in a more restrained style in keeping with the Dutch King's conservative sensibilities. William and Mary were avid gardeners, and so a 26-acre formal garden was laid out in the grounds around the palace. The Royal Family

The Sunken Gardens behind Kensington Palace.

moved into the palace in time to celebrate Christmas in 1689. Queen Mary died of smallpox here in 1694. Eight years later, her husband died here after a hunting accident at Hampton Court. When Mary's younger sister, Anne, took the throne, she had Christopher Wren add the Orangery, and expanded the gardens. In 1702, Anne died at Kensington Palace, bringing to an end the Stuart Dynasty.

The crown then passed to the House of Hanover. George I came to London with his extended entourage of German retainers and courtiers and moved into Kensington Palace. George I and George II redecorated the palace and added elaborate ceiling decorations in the Privy Chamber, Cupola Room, and the King's Grand Staircase. The commission was first offered to the official court painter, Sir James Thornhill, but the frugal King thought Thornhill's bid was too high. The commission went to the little-known artist William Kent, who established his reputation with his work at Kensington Palace. In 1760, George II died in the palace, after which the palace was never again used as a residence by the monarch.

George III's fourth son, Edward, Duke of Kent, moved into Kensington Palace, where his daughter, the future Queen Victoria was born on May 24, 1819. After her father died, Victoria was brought up in Kensington Palace by her strict mother. In the early morning hours of June 20, 1837, the Lord Chamberlain and the Archbishop of Canterbury came to Kensington Palace to bring the news to the 18-year-old Alexandrina Victoria that her uncle, William IV, had died and she was the new Queen. Almost immediately Victoria moved into Buckingham Palace, even before its renovations were completed. The Queen never again stayed at Kensington Palace, but she opened the gardens and State Apartments to the public.

Kensington Palace in London has remained a Royal Residence for members of the extended Royal Family. Royals jokingly refer to the palace as the "Aunt Heap." Kensington Palace has offices and private apartments for Princess Alice (widow of the late Duke of Gloucester), and her son and daughter-in-law (the present Duke and Duchess of Gloucester), the Duke and Duchess of Kent, and Prince and Princess Michael of Kent. Before their deaths both Princess Margaret and Diana, Princess of Wales, used to live in Kensington Palace and had their offices there. The Princess of Wales occupied apartments in the northwest part of Kensington Palace from 1981 to 1997. After Diana's death, crowds coming to London for her funeral grew so massive that her coffin was taken from the Chapel Royal in St. James's Palace to Kensington Palace so the funeral procession could be extended to accommodate the mass of mourners who lined the route from Kensington Palace to Westminster Abbey.

Planning Your Visit

Purchase your ticket and pick up the audio guide, which is included with your admission fee. First take a tour of the Royal Dress Collection, which displays clothing worn by members of the Royal Family, including coronation robes, wedding dresses, and a collection of dresses, hats, and handbags belonging to Queen Elizabeth II. The highlight of the collection is a display of fourteen fabulous evening gowns worn by Diana, Princess of Wales. The audio guide tends to be tedious for the main Dress Collection, but is excellent for the Diana Collection and is essential for exploring the rest of the Royal Apartments.

After you view the Royal Dress Collection, visit the Royal Apartments, which are furnished with spectacular items from the Royal Collection. You can see the suite of rooms used by Princess Victoria and her mother, the Duchess of Kent, in the early 19th century. The rooms are furnished with many items that belonged to the future Queen. The self-guided tour includes the grand Cupola Room, where the infant Victoria was baptized, and the Presence Chamber with its magnificent ceiling painted by William Kent and elaborate woodcarvings by Grinling Gibbons. The King's Grand Staircase, painted by William Kent, presents a gallery of George I's colorful entourage, including the figures of the King's two Turkish grooms, Mahomet and Mustapha, and Peter "the wild boy," who was found in the woods near Hanover after supposedly being raised by animals.

After you conclude your tour of the interior, make sure you see the 18th-century sunken gardens behind Kensington Palace. Standing outside the east front of the palace is a statue of Queen Victoria sculpted by her fourth daughter, Princess Louise, who had a studio at Kensington Palace. To mark her mother's Golden Jubilee in 1887, Louise carved this fine marble statue of Queen Victoria as she appeared at the time of her accession.

Opening hours

November 1 - February 28: Open daily 10:00 a.m. - 5:00 p.m. (last admission: 4:00 p.m.) (closed December 24-26, January 1, Good Friday and other official holidays).

March 1 - October 31: Open daily 10:00 a.m. - 6:00 p.m. (last admission: 5:00 p.m.).

The stylish Orangery Café located beside Kensington Palace serves light lunches and snacks and is open throughout the year.

To purchase tickets

On-line

Go to www.hrp.org.uk.

By telephone

Credit card sales: (0) 870 751 5180

In person

Tickets can be purchased on the day of your visit at the ticket desk. Follow the signs from the main entrance gate. Combination Tickets allowing entry to Hampton Court, Tower of London, and Kensington Palace can be purchased at their respective ticket offices.

Getting there

By Underground

Kensington Palace is located at the western end of Kensington Gardens and can be reached by Underground at either the High Street Kensington or Queensway Tube station. The High Street Kensington Tube station is served by the Circle and District Lines. As you exit the High Street Kensington Tube station, you enter a small shopping arcade. Walk straight through the shopping center onto Kensington High Street and turn to the right. Kensington Palace is about a 15-minute walk from the Kensington High Street Tube station. After you walk two blocks, you will see the gates to the garden across the street over to your left. Cross at the crosswalk and enter through the first set of small gates at the corner of Kensington High Street and Palace Avenue, which will lead to the ornate main gate on the south side of the palace. Kensington Palace can also be reached on the Central Line from the

Queensway Tube station. As you exit the station onto Queensway, turn right and walk the few steps to the corner of Bayswater Road. Cross at the crosswalk and turn right. (A public restroom will be located across the road to the left of the crosswalk.) Walk the short distance to the Broad Walk entrance to Kensington Gardens. Turn left to enter the gardens, where you will see the new Princess Diana Memorial Children's Playground on your right. Walk further down Broad Walk past the children's playground. You will find the palace on the right further ahead. Again follow the signs, which will take you to the entrance of the palace.

By bus

Kensington Palace may be reached on bus routes 12 and 94 to Bayswater Road or 9, 10, 27, 28, 49, 52, 52A, 70, 328 and C1 to Kensington High Street.

♦ Greenwich Palace

Although Greenwich Palace saw its glory days as a Royal Palace during the 16th century, when Henry VIII and his daughters, Mary and Elizabeth, ruled England, the wood-timbered Tudor buildings have long been replaced by the classical buildings designed by Inigo Jones and Christopher Wren for the Stuart dynasty. Greenwich is only five miles outside central London. You can easily spend the day exploring its museums, strolling its beautifully landscaped parks, and enjoying the picturesque town.

History of Greenwich Palace

Greenwich has been a Royal Residence since the time of Edward I in 1300. King Henry V granted the manor to his Lord Chancellor, Thomas Beaufort, Duke of Exeter. Later it passed to Humphrey, Duke of Gloucester, who became regent and protector of his young nephew, Henry VI. In 1433, Humphrey enclosed 200 acres of land as a park and hunting preserve—the first Royal Park. After Humphrey's death in 1447, the manor reverted to his nephew, Henry VI, who renamed the palace *Placentia* (meaning "the Pleasant Place").

When King Henry VII took the throne, he sent the palace's occupant, Elizabeth, the widowed Queen of Edward IV, to a nunnery, and converted the manor house into one of his Royal Residences. Henry VIII was born here on June 28, 1491. Henry VIII made Greenwich his primary residence. On June 3, 1509, Henry married his brother's widow, Catherine of Aragon, at the nearby Greyfriars' Church. Their daughter, Mary, the future queen, was born at Greenwich in 1516. Henry VIII dreamed of a mighty English navy

160

Greenwich Palace as viewed across the Thames from the Isle of Dogs.

and built the Royal Dockyard along the Thames. Greenwich soon became the maritime capital of England.

Henry courted his second wife, Anne Boleyn, at Greenwich and their daughter, Princess Elizabeth, was born here. Three years after Elizabeth's birth, her mother, Anne Boleyn, was arrested at Greenwich and was taken to the Tower of London, where she was beheaded. In 1540, Henry VIII first met his fourth bride, Anne of Cleves, who arrived at Greenwich for their short-lived marriage.

Henry's heir and successor, Edward VI, lived at Greenwich during his 5-year reign before he died here in 1553 at age 15. Queen Elizabeth I regularly held court at Greenwich. It is said that Elizabeth was walking the grounds of Greenwich when the courtier Sir Walter Raleigh gallantly threw his cloak over a puddle so the Queen would not get her feet wet. In 1587, Elizabeth was at Greenwich when she signed the death warrant for her Catholic cousin, Mary, Queen of Scots. Elizabeth knighted Sir Francis Drake on board his ship, the *Golden Hinde*, when Drake returned to Greenwich after sailing around the world.

Elizabeth's successor, James I, and his Queen, Anne of Denmark, engaged Inigo Jones in 1616 to build the Queen's House in the new Palladian style midway up the hill from the Thames. It was completed by Charles I, who gave the house to his young French wife, Queen Henrietta Maria. After Charles I was executed in the English Civil War, the palace was used as a prison and a biscuit factory during Cromwell's Protectorate. After the Restoration, Charles II resumed construction of the new palace under Inigo Jones's son-in-law, John Webb. Charles's grandiose building schemes were hampered by a continual lack of funds. Only the old Royal Observatory at the top of the hill and one wing of the new palace were completed before the funds ran out. It was not until the reign of William and Mary that the palace as we see it today began to take shape.

In 1694, Queen Mary directed Christopher Wren and his assistant, Nicholas Hawksmoor, to turn the palace into the Greenwich Hospital for retired

View of the Queen's House *(foreground)* and the old Royal Observatory *(top of the hill).*

sailors. Wren demolished the remaining old-fashioned Tudor buildings and built the second parallel wing of the palace on the other side of the grounds, framing the Queen's House in the center so as not to obstruct the Queen's river view. Mary died of smallpox later that year and never lived to see her pet project completed. Wren's Greenwich Hospital for retired sailors became the Royal Naval College in 1837, and the Chapel and Painted Hall were opened to the public. The Royal Naval College closed in 1989 and the property was given to the University of Greenwich and the Trinity College of Music.

Planning Your Visit

There is much to see and do at Greenwich. If at all possible, try to come during the week, as the weekends can be impossibly crowded with hordes of tourists and locals visiting the museums and the popular weekend crafts and antique markets in town. When you arrive at Greenwich, go to the Tourist Information Centre located in the Pepys House on the palace grounds just behind the ship *Cutty Sark*. Check out the Centre's free exhibit on the history of Greenwich, which displays the layout of the former palace and park grounds. The Centre also has a small café and public restrooms. Guided tours are offered by the Greenwich Tour Guides Association. The tours depart from just outside the Tourist Information Centre twice daily at 12:15 p.m. and 2:15 p.m.

Begin your visit at the magnificent Painted Hall—the former dining hall for veteran sailors, opulently decorated with the paintings of Sir James Thornhill celebrating the reign of William and Mary. Cross the courtyard to see the eye-catching Chapel of Sts. Peter and Paul. The chapel was originally designed by Christopher Wren, but was extensively restored by James "Athenian" Stuart after a fire in 1779. The chapel contains the enormous painting *The Preservation of St. Paul after Shipwreck at Malta*, by the American-born artist Benjamin West.

Visit the National Maritime Museum, which claims to be the world's largest nautical museum. It was opened to the public by George VI on April 27, 1937. Not just for would-be mariners, this museum has state-of-the-art displays on British naval history and exploration with uniforms, nautical instruments, and countless model boats as well as the full-size royal barge of Frederick, Prince of Wales, eldest son of George II, who died before taking the throne. Do not miss the exhibition on the life and times of Lord Horatio Nelson. An entire wing of the museum is devoted in tribute to the "immortal memory" of this maritime hero of the Napoleonic Wars. The exhibit has many fascinating objects from Lord Nelson's life, including the bloodied uniform Nelson was wearing when he died from a sniper's bullet during the climactic Battle of Trafalgar.

Inigo Jones's Palladian-styled Queen's House is a part of the National Maritime Museum. It is the earliest of Jones's architectural masterworks. The Great Hall in the Queen's House is a perfect 40-foot cube, and the house has a stunning spiral "tulip staircase." Unfortunately, the beautiful house is filled with rather boring paintings, but is worth a quick peek for the striking interior architecture.

After you visit the Queen's House, pass through the Greenwich Park flower gardens and climb the hill to the old Royal Observatory, which is also a part of the National Maritime Museum. The observatory was built by Christopher Wren in 1675 for John Flamsteed, the first Astronomer Royal. Charles II recognized the British Navy's need to determine longitude—one's precise position east and west—while at sea and out of sight of land. The 0° longitude mark dividing the eastern and western hemispheres was established passing through Greenwich between the old Royal Observatory and Flamsteed House. Since 1884, time has been measured from the Greenwich Meridian Line at the old Royal Observatory. Greenwich Mean Time (GMT) is the standard measurement of time worldwide. You can visit Flamsteed House, the old Royal Observatory, and the Meridian building, which houses a huge collection of clocks, astronomical instruments, and chronometers. From the top of the hill, standing next to the statue of General James Wolfe, there are superb views over the grounds of Greenwich Palace, along the Thames, past the Docklands, and all the way to modern London in the distance.

Down by the river, near the Greenwich Pier, you can visit the *Cutty Sark*, the last surviving tea-clipper. Nearby is the small *Gipsy Moth IV*, which Sir Francis Chichester sailed single-handedly around the world in 1966-67. He was knighted by Queen Elizabeth II, using the same sword with which Elizabeth I had honored Sir Frances Drake for his circumnavigation of the world. Beside the Greenwich Pier you will also see a small, domed building. There you will find a foot tunnel, which runs under the Thames and leads to the Isle of Dogs, where you can enjoy spectacular views of Greenwich Palace.

Take time to look around the town of Greenwich, which is filled with charming antique shops, bookstores, covered markets, restaurants, and taverns. The Church of St. Alfege is dedicated to the former Archbishop of Canterbury, who was captured by a raiding party of Danes in 1012 and put to death here. A church was erected on the site of his martyrdom. It was used as a royal chapel during Tudor times, and the infant Henry VIII was baptized there. The current church, designed by Nicholas Hawksmoor, was rebuilt in 1718. It has fine interior woodwork by Grinling Gibbons and elaborate iron rails by Jean Tijou. The church contains the tombs of General James Wolfe, who died fighting the French in Quebec in 1759, and of 16th-century composer and organist Thomas Tallis.

Opening hours

Painted Hall and Chapel
Admission free; Open Monday – Saturday 10:00 a.m. - 5:00 p.m.; Sunday 12:30 p.m. - 5:00 p.m. (last admission 4:00 p.m.). The public is welcome to attend the Sunday services offered at 11:00 a.m.

National Maritime Museum
Admission is free, but there may be charges to attend some special exhibitions; National Maritime Museum, the Queen's House and old Royal Observatory open daily 10:00 a.m. - 5:00 p.m. (until 6:00 p.m. July - August) (closed December 24-26, January 1). The last admissions are 30 minutes before closing. Check out the National Maritime Museum's Web site, www.nmm.ac.uk.

Cutty Sark Museum

Open Monday – Saturday 10:00 a.m.- 5:00 p.m.; Sunday 12:00 p.m. - 5:00 p.m. (6:00 p.m. July - August).

Getting there

By riverboat

You can board the riverboats that will take you to Greenwich Pier from London's Westminster Pier (near the Houses of Parliament), Charing Cross Pier (along the Embankment), or the Tower Pier (near the Tower of London). The riverboats depart for Greenwich Pier approximately every 30 minutes from May - October and every 45 minutes from November - April. The boat trip takes about 45 minutes, depending on the tides. Check to make sure when the last return boat departs—usually at 5:45 p.m. from June - August and at 3:45 p.m. during the rest of the year.

By Underground

The Underground is the least desirable option to reach Greenwich. The new Jubilee Line extension will take you to the North Greenwich Tube station (by the ill-fated Millennium Dome) where you can catch Bus No. 188 to Greenwich, or you can get off at the previous stop–Canary Wharf Tube station—and change to the Docklands Light Railway for the trip into Greenwich. It makes better sense to simply take the Docklands Light Railway all the way.

By Docklands Light Railway

The easiest way to reach Greenwich is by London's convenient Docklands Light Railway (the "DLR"). The new computer-driven light railcars run every 10-15 minutes from London's Bank Tube station down to the *Cutty Sark* Tube station (near the Greenwich Pier) or the next stop, Greenwich Tube station (near the National Maritime Museum). The DLR offers spectacular views along the way of London's new futuristic Docklands development and Canary Wharf Tower.

By train

Regular train service to Greenwich is provided by Connex South Eastern and departs from either the Charing Cross or Waterloo train stations. Get off at the Greenwich station if you want to explore the town, or wait for the next stop at Maze Hill located next to the National Maritime Museum. The trip from Charing Cross to Maze Hill takes about 20 minutes.

By bus

You may reach Greenwich by bus No. 188, which runs between Russell Square and Greenwich via Waterloo and makes the trip in 35 minutes depending on the traffic.

CHAPTER 7
GETTING AROUND LONDON

London is huge and can be daunting to the first-time visitor. While there, you should always carry a good map of the city and its Underground system. Even experienced Londoners need to refer to a map from time to time. During your stay, you will inevitably run across bewildered travelers pouring over their maps trying to figure out where they are and where they are going. The city evolved from a collection of small villages. The original one square mile of the old City of London that grew up within the confines of its old Roman walls has now swelled into a megalopolis that stretches for 620 square miles. The resulting jumbled layout of streets can be very confusing. When exiting from an Underground station, you should refer to your map to re-orient yourself before moving on.

Dorling Kindersley's *Travel Guides Series London City Map* and the *Streetwise London* are both good choices. You can buy your map before you leave, or you can find maps for sale at the main British Tourist Centre on Regent Street, at local bookstores, from vending machines in the Underground stations, and at souvenir shops. You should buy a plastic laminated map, which will hold up better in London's frequently wet weather. The free maps handed out by hotels are made of flimsy paper and tend to disintegrate rather quickly even in dry conditions. Invest in a good map and always carry it with you. You will be glad you did.

The second thing you will want to keep with you at all times during your stay in London is an umbrella (called "brollies" by the Brits). The weather in London is very changeable. Britain is an island. Weather fronts can move through quickly. You can have clear blue skies in the morning and then have rain showers off and on all afternoon, or you can start out with soggy skies and end up with a glorious afternoon. Always carry a small collapsible umbrella with you, just in case!

London on foot

The tours in this guide explore the central areas around the Palace of Westminster, Whitehall, Trafalgar Square, Piccadilly, St. James's, and Buckingham Palace. These areas can easily be reached by the Underground and explored on foot. Getting around London can be tricky at first for the pedestrian, because the British drive on the left side of the street. For many people, looking before you cross a street is almost a reflex. You must be

166

very careful. Even after several days in England, many visitors tend to look the wrong way when they step onto the street. The routes traveled on the tours in this guide take you through some of the most popular and traffic-congested areas of London. When you come to a street crossing while taking any tour, remember to always push the pause button on your CD player. Take off your CD earphones and look both ways before you cross the street. When you push the play button, your CD player will pick up the narration where you left off.

London's popular black taxi and signature red double-decker bus.

Recently, London has invested heavily in streetscaping its main tourist areas. The authorities have tried to establish clearly marked pedestrian crossings on the busiest streets. The crossings on many streets are indicated with white zebra stripes, and the streets are sometimes marked "look left" or "look right" near the curb to remind you which way to look before you step out onto the street. Railings have been installed along the streets at a number of heavily traveled areas to encourage the pedestrians to cross only at the designated spots. Railed pedestrian islands have been set up in the middle of many busy roads for your added protection.

London by Public Transportation

London offers a variety of transportation options that can be a bit confusing to the first-time visitor. Transport for London (TfL) is a newly formed executive body of the Greater London Authority (GLA), which reports to the Mayor of London. The TfL was created to manage and integrate the public transportation system, including London's Underground system, London's bus system, the Docklands Light Railway (DLR), the National Rail trains, and the developing London River Services (LRS). Like any modern city, getting anywhere in the city during rush hour (weekdays between 8:00 a.m. and 9:30 a.m. and between 4:30 p.m. and 6:30 p.m.) can be a nightmare. If at all possible, try to avoid traveling on the public transportation system during these times. The only time I would recommend braving London's early morning rush hour is on a visit to the Tower of London, where it pays to be there when the gates open to avoid the normal crush.

Tube stations usually display the exit to most important sites.

Remember to "mind the gap" as you board your train.

Over 8.5 million trips are made each day on the aging infrastructure of the public transportation system of Greater London. The system is being revamped to try to cope with the increased traffic. Parts of the public transportation system, including the London Underground, are being privatized and will be run by several different operators under the oversight of the TfL. Inevitably, some of the transportation information in this guide will be overtaken by the rapid changes that are being implemented. For the most up-to-date information, you may want to check out the TfL Web site, www.londontransport.co.uk.

London by the Underground "Tube"

To reach the destinations explored in this guide, the Underground system is the best option. The Underground is generally much faster than buses or taxis, but it can be uncomfortably crowded during rush hours. Most of the Underground lines run daily (except Christmas) from 5:30 a.m. until midnight Monday through Saturday, and 7:30 a.m. to 11:30 p.m. on Sunday. Before you leave, you can check out your connections and available service on the Tubeplanner at the Underground's Web site, www.thetube.com, or you can check the information posted at the station nearest your hotel to confirm the time for the last train service at that station.

At the beginning of most tours in this guide, directions for the starting point will be given from the nearest Tube station. London's transportation system dates back to 1863 with the opening of the world's first underground railway. The Londoners call the subway the "Underground" or the "Tube" even though portions of many routes run above ground. Only the Victoria, Waterloo, and City lines run entirely underground. Be aware that in Britain "subway" refers to an under-the-street pedestrian walkway and not the underground train system. The vast network of trains covers most corners of this enormous city and enables you to get from place to place, usually with convenient connections. As the gridlocked traffic has slowed surface travel by bus or taxi to a crawl, the Tube has become the fastest way to get around.

The Underground system has 12 color-coded lines, which are accessible by 273 Tube stations, and covers 253 miles of railway. Tube stations are easily identified by the signs with their blue line and red-circled logo. The twelve Tube lines are:

Bakerloo (brown)
Central (red)
Circle (yellow)
District (green)
East London (orange)
Hammersmith & City (pink)
Jubilee (silver)
Metropolitan (purple)
Northern (black)
Piccadilly (dark blue)
Victoria (light blue)
Waterloo & City (light green)

The Circle Line (yellow) runs in a loop around central London, while the other lines cross the city. The Piccadilly Line (dark blue), the Jubilee Line (silver), and the Northern Line (black) cross through the center of the areas explored in *Royal London In Context*.

When you first enter or exit a Tube station, you will find helpful "Journey Planner" maps on the wall showing each stop in the line's route. The map indicates the stations where you can change to another line to reach your intended destination. A double circle linking the different-colored lines on the map means that the station connects between two or more lines. When you get off the train, look for the signs directing you to the connecting lines or to the exit (marked the "Way Out").

Inside each station, you can find self-service ticket machines with easy-to-follow instructions for purchasing your tickets. The machines will offer single (one-way) tickets, return (round-trip) tickets, or one-day Travelcards with separate fares for adults and for children. Some machines take bills or

Tube ticket machine.

coins and give change, while others require exact change. There are also ticket windows where you can buy your ticket or Travelcard and where you may ask the helpful staff for information on how to get to your destination.

Greater London is divided into six travel zones, which are laid out in six concentric circles radiating out from the inner city, which is Zone 1. The ticket fares on London's public transportation, including the Underground, the buses, and trains, are based on the number of zones in which you travel. The twelve tours in this guide and most of the sites of historical interest to London tourists are found within Zone 1. Most visitors stay within Zones 1 and 2. Zone 6 extends far into the suburbs—called "Greater London"—and goes all the way to Heathrow Airport, which is linked to the city on the Piccadilly Line.

A bewildering variety of frequently changing fares and combinations of travel tickets and discount cards are offered that can challenge the patience of even seasoned travelers. There are Day Travelcards, Weekend Travelcards, Family Travelcards, a Carnet (book of ten single tickets that can each be used for only one trip), and there are passes for travel during peak and off-peak periods, and a range of one-day and multi-day bus passes. Ticket offices in the Tube and railway stations offer a brochure that attempts to explain the confusing array of ticket options you can consider.

Each single ticket is valid for one trip only. If you want to buy a round-trip ticket, get a "return ticket." A single Zone 1 ticket is good for only one trip and may be used only on the day of purchase. The book of ten tickets (the "Carnet") is good for twelve months from the date of purchase. The Carnet is cheaper than buying ten separate tickets. Each ticket is valid for a single, one-way trip within Zone 1, but may not be used on the Docklands Light Railway (DLR).

If you are going to use public transportation to take two or more trips during your visit, your best bet is to buy one of the Travelcards, which can be bought for one or more days of travel, depending on how long you will be in London. It is cheaper and avoids the inconvenience of standing in line

The ticket turnstile at a Tube station.

(referred to in Britain as "queuing up"). The Travelcards may be used on the Tube, train, light rail, or bus system in the zone or zones you have selected. Holders of Travelcards also get a discount on some river transport lines. Your ticket or Travelcard must authorize travel in all the zones covered in your journey. You may not exit in a zone outside of the zone authorized by your ticket or Travelcard, or you will be assessed a hefty penalty. The machine at the exit will alert the staff if you try to exit outside your authorized zones.

Forget about trying to make sense of the Byzantine maze of ticket offers and combinations. Unless you are in London for only a short time and intend to rely on taxis and walking, go ahead a buy a one-day Travelcard for Zones 1 and 2 (unless you plan on going to the outskirts of London, then you should get the 6-Zone card) or buy a Carnet with ten single trip tickets for travel within Zones 1 and 2. The one-day Travelcard can be used to make unlimited trips within your selected zones. To lessen the crush of the early morning rush hour during the work week, the one-day Travelcard may only be used after 9:30 a.m. from Monday to Friday, but it can be used all day during weekends, and on public holidays. It is not valid on Night Buses. If you are going to be in London only over the weekend, you can buy a Weekend Travelcard.

If you will be in London for an entire week, go ahead and buy a seven-day Travelcard, which will give you unlimited travel throughout the selected zones for seven days, and includes the use of Night Buses. To buy a seven-day Travelcard, you will need a passport-size photograph. If you forget to bring a passport photo with you, you can find automatic photo machines in the railway stations and in major Tube stations, where you can get a snapshot that will do nicely.

Another option to consider is the London Pass, which is a 6-Zone Travelcard that also provides entry to over 60 popular London attractions, and offers various discounts. The London Pass also allows you to jump to the front of the lines at many attractions. The London Pass can be bought for 1, 2, 3, or 6 days with or without public transportation. For more details, check its Web site, www.londonpass.com.

Once you have purchased your ticket or Travelcard, proceed to the bank of turnstiles. Insert your ticket or Travelcard face up and magnetic strip

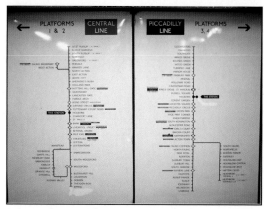

Route signs in Tube station serving the Central and Piccadilly Lines.

down in the marked slot on the right side of the machine. The card should pass through and pop up on the top. When you remove your ticket from the top of the machine, the gate will open so you can pass through. Remember to retrieve your ticket! You will need to repeat the process at the turnstiles you will find at the exit of each Tube station. Always hold on to your ticket or Travelcard during your trip. If you are stopped by an Underground inspector and fail to show your ticket or Travelcard you will be fined on the spot.

London is switching over to the so-called "smart card" for use in the London Underground and in the rest of the city's public transportation system. The smart cards use an ID chip and will eventually replace the old magnetic-strip cards. The chip in the smart cards eliminates the need for travelers to insert the cards in a slot. Instead, the card is waved over a card reader placed at the top of the turnstile gate or bus entry point.

In Tube stations that serve more than one line, you will see signs directing you to the appropriate line. The different trains on each line are identified by the last stop on their routes. When in doubt, refer to your map of the Tube system in this guide or on the maps that are displayed at various points in each station and on the trains. You will generally have to take one or more sets of escalators to reach the lower level and the Underground train platforms. The Underground system is 221 feet below street level at its deepest point (at the Hampstead Heath station). In some stations you will take an elevator (called the "lift" in Britain) down to the platform. The escalators in the Tube stations are huge! When you step onto the escalator, stand to the right to let those in a hurry pass by. Enjoy the signs on the walls to your right, which advertise the latest West End shows, or watch the fascinating passing parade of humanity going in the opposite direction on your left.

Once you reach the lower level, you will see signs directing you to the platforms on the right or left depending on the direction in which you wish to travel. The sign will identify the line and the direction in which the train is traveling, and will list each of the stops the train will make. The same sign will be repeated on the wall opposite the platform. Many stations now have elec-

Escalator leading down to Piccadilly Line platform.

tronic indicator boards displaying the end destination of the next oncoming train and the estimated time you will have to wait until the next train arrives. The sign on the front of the train will indicate the last stop made by the train on this route.

When the train arrives, stand back as the passengers get off and hurry off to the "Way Out." Once you board the train, you will see a chart showing each stop along the train's route and an Underground map showing you the overall system. When your train reaches each station along the way, you will see the name of the station on the wall. On many trains, a recorded announcement will advise you of the upcoming stations. As your train reaches the station, you may hear the ubiquitous announcement that has amused foreign tourists for years—"mind the gap"—warning you to take care when you get off as there may be a slight space between the train door and the train platform. On some trains you will need to push a button on the side of the door to open the carriage door.

When you get off the train, look for the "Way Out" sign or the sign indicating the way to the platform for your connecting line. If you are exiting, you will have to take a few stairs, and either several sets of escalators or an elevator (the "lift") up to the street level. Once you reach the street level, you will come to another set of turnstiles where you will repeat the process of inserting your ticket or Travelcard into the slot or waving your smart card by the sensor. Again, do not forget to retrieve your multi-use ticket or Travelcard. After you pass through the turnstile, you can find a map on the station wall marked "Continuing your Journey," which provides a detailed view of the immediate area, and identifies the important nearby sites and connecting bus lines. If you have any questions about which line to take or what connection to use, look for the helpful Transport officer in the station (recognizable by their trademark blue cap) or just ask for assistance at the ticket window.

London, like any big city, has crime. Be especially alert for pickpockets when using the Underground and keep your valuables safe. Thieves like to take advantage of the confusing rush of the crowds. Unless you are in a group, avoid traveling on the Underground late at night. If you use a Night Bus late at night, stay in the bottom level, where you can see the driver. When in doubt, be safe and take a taxi.

London by Bus

The old-fashioned, bright red, double-decker buses still ply the streets of London. Even though the traffic-clogged roads can make the trip a frustrating experience if you are in a hurry, riding on the top of a double-decker bus can offer an interesting view of the city. The London bus system can seem confusing. The bus lines are marked by their route number, and the major destinations for each bus are listed on the window on the front of the bus. All bus stops have diagrams showing the route numbers of the bus lines that stop there, and the signs show the stops each bus makes along its designated route. However, the names of most stops are unfamiliar to most first-time visitors. There is also a frequency guide showing how often the bus line stops at the bus stop. The buses regularly stop at the stops marked with a red horizontal stripe through the red circle. Some bus stop signs are marked with "Request" on the stripe through the red circle, which means that the buses do not automatically stop there. You must raise your arm to signal the bus driver to stop if you want to board. The newer buses board from the front, and you can

The old-fashioned double-decker bus boards from the rear.

174

buy a single ticket from the driver as you enter. The older-style buses have both a driver and a conductor and can be boarded from the open rear platform. The conductor will come around and collect your fare.

You cannot buy a Travelcard on board the bus. The single ticket is only valid for the one journey on that one bus. If you change buses, you will need to buy another ticket. Keep your ticket with you until you reach your destination. You can confirm with the driver or conductor if this bus goes to your intended destination, and you can ask where you should get off.

Be careful and hold on as you walk down the aisle to take your seat or when climbing the stairs to the upper deck of the bus. The ride can be quite bumpy and the bus may stop suddenly. For your safety, standing is not permitted. Pay attention to the progress of your bus trip. If you are enjoying the view from the upper deck, give yourself plenty of time to make your way back downstairs to get off at your destination. Buses do not always halt at each stop if there is no one standing by the sign. Remember to ring the bell as your stop approaches. Be careful to disembark only at designated stops, even though you may see Londoners hopping off between stops.

London also has a Night Bus service that runs all night. You can get a bus ride back to the vicinity of your hotel, departing from Trafalgar Square. The lines are marked with an N and then the route number. The Night Buses only run about once an hour on most routes. At night, when the bus service is reduced, hailing a taxi is a safer way to get back to your hotel.

In London there are many private bus tours, including the Big Bus Tour and the Original Bus Tour, offering "hop on, hop off" service to the main tourist areas in London. For one flat daily fee, you can jump off to visit a tourist site and then catch the next bus that comes along, or you can stay on the bus and get a driving tour of the city. The private bus tours are far more expensive than using the local transit system. They offer no interaction with real Londoners and can often get bogged down in London's notorious traffic, but they are convenient and can provide a good overview of the city's major attractions.

Sightseeing buses are a popular option to see the city.

London by Docklands Light Railway

The Docklands Light Railway (DLR) runs from the Bank Tube station or Tower Gateway near the Tower Hill Tube station (both served by the District and Circle Underground Lines) through the Docklands and Canary Wharf towards Greenwich. The DLR service runs from 5:30 a.m. until about 12:30 a.m. (Monday through Saturday) and 7:00 a.m. until 11:30 p.m. on Sunday.

London's newest transportation option, the DLR.

London by Train

London's trains arrive at Charing Cross, Euston, King's Cross, Paddington, Victoria, Waterloo, and Liverpool Street stations. If you plan on visiting Windsor Castle, you will depart from either Paddington or Waterloo Station. Hampton Court is reached by train departing from the Waterloo Station. Greenwich Palace may be reached by trains departing from either the Charing Cross or London Waterloo train station, but the new Docklands Light Rail is the best way to reach Greenwich. The Eurostar train to Paris departs from Waterloo. King's Cross station provides service for most of northeastern England and Scotland. Trains from Paddington reach the western and southwestern parts of England.

When you reach the train station you will need to go to the ticket window and ask for a round-trip or "return ticket" to and from your destination. Ask at the window for the next departure time and the number of the platform where you will board your train. This information will also be

London's easy commuter train service.

posted on overhead boards in the central hall of the station. Play it safe and ask at the ticket window and then confirm the information with the overhead board. You can also purchase train tickets from automatic machines similar to those in Underground stations.

Train stations offer both automated ticket machines and staffed ticket desks.

The train destination is also usually displayed on the electronic message board at the platform. An electronic message board in each railway car displays each stop. Also, the name of the train station is clearly posted at each stop on the platform. If you are still in doubt, feel free to double-check with the friendly uniformed train crewmember before you board. A uniformed conductor will pass through the rail car to stamp or verify the validity of your train ticket or pass. Check out the British train Web sites, www.britrail.com and www.railtrack.co.uk.

London by Taxi

A ride in one of London's landmark taxicabs is a quintessential London experience, but they are a relatively expensive way to travel around in London, unless you are in a group of three or more. The taxi fare is based on the time and not the number of passengers. Be aware that in the congestion of rush-hour traffic, the Tube will be a cheaper and quicker way to reach your destination.

The official taxis no longer have to be the traditional black, and many are now decked out with multicolored advertisements. The traditional taxi comes with two fold-down seats behind the driver and can accommodate up to five passengers. The interior is spacious and has a high dome so that passengers wearing bowler hats can be seated comfortably. The drivers of the officially licensed "black cabs" are famous for their mastery of "The Knowledge" of London streets. Taxi drivers have to devote several years of study and practice to absorb the detailed and intimate knowledge of the London streets, traffic patterns, and quickest routes required to pass the test and get a license.

You can hail a taxi by stepping off the curb with your hand raised. You can also find taxi stands located in front of major hotels and near some of London's principal attractions. You can order a taxi by telephone, but there is an extra charge. If the yellow sign above the windshield is illuminated, it means the taxi is available. If you don't see a yellow sign at all, then it is not a licensed taxi, but rather a minicab. The minicabs are unlicensed and can look like regular cars. You can make arrangements to order a minicab by telephone. They are not supposed to pick up passengers on the streets, but often do so, particularly late at night. They have no meters. If you choose a minicab, you will need to negotiate your fare before you board. Unlike licensed taxis, the minicabs undergo no regular inspection and may or may not be properly insured.

You can tell your taxi driver where you want to go and ask what the approximate cost of the journey will be before you start your trip. When you reach your destination, get out first and pay the driver through the side window. It is customary to add a tip of about 10% of the fare. Many taxi drivers are quite colorful characters and can provide interesting tidbits about the London scene.

If you have taken the Gatwick Express, Thameslink or the Heathrow Express from the airport into central London, you would be better off taking a taxi from the train station to your hotel rather than taking the Underground. Particularly if you arrive in morning rush hour (before 9:30 a.m.), it will be very difficult trying to haul your luggage up and down the series of stairs and escalators and through connecting halls with the crush of business commuters. People are usually tired after a long transatlantic flight. Relax and use the taxi ride from the station to your hotel to orient yourself to London.

London by London River Services (LRS)

London River Services Limited (LRS) was set up in 1997 as a subsidiary of London for Transport and is charged with the goal of developing a river passenger service. Daily riverboat service is offered from central London piers, including Westminster, the Tower of London, Millbank Millennium, and Bankside east up the Thames to and from Greenwich, and, in summers, from central London west out to Hampton Court Palace. Tickets can be purchased at the piers, and, in some cases, on board. The system is still under development with a number of providers, and the service varies with the season. Stop by the ticket office at one of the piers along the Thames to check for current times, fares, and destinations.

CHAPTER 8
ARRIVING IN LONDON

Getting to and From London's Main Airports

London's two main airports for international travelers are Heathrow (LHR) and Gatwick (LGW). The other three London area airports—Stansted, Luton, and London City Airport—primarily serve airlines that offer connecting service within Europe.

International Airport Arrival Procedures

The initial arrival procedures for international visitors are generally the same at both Heathrow and Gatwick international airports. Most often the international flights disembark directly from the plane into the terminal. On some planes you must disembark onto the tarmac, where you will board buses that will take you into the terminal. When you first enter the terminal, you will have to go through passport control. You should have received a passport entry form to fill out during your flight. If you did not get one from the flight attendant, additional forms are available at a table located before you reach the passport control booths. Remember to have the form completed before you reach passport control.

When lining up to go through passport control, note that there are separate passport control lines for citizens of Britain and other European Union ("EU") countries, and for citizens of the US and other non-EU countries. Look for the signs indicating which lines are for the US and other non-EU citizens. After you pass through passport control, follow the signs to the baggage claim area, where you can retrieve your luggage. Overhead monitors will indicate where to find your flight's luggage. Luggage trolleys are available to help if you have a number of bags to manage. Once you have collected your luggage, follow the signs to the customs area. There are spot checks and security checks. Once you pass through the customs area, you will then enter the main airport. Look for the signs indicating the way to the transportation area to select your means of getting into central London.

Gatwick Airport

Gatwick Airport is located about 28 miles south of London. It has a North and South Terminal. Check your ticket to see whether you are arriving in Gatwick's South or North Terminal. The main transportation links to London are located in the South Terminal. If you have arrived in the North

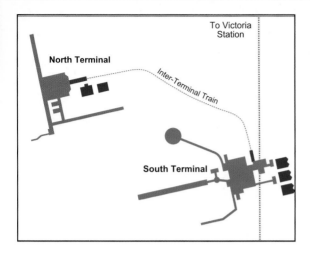

Terminal, you can quickly get to the South Terminal by taking the free monorail that runs every few minutes between the terminals. For more information on the airport and its services, visit the airport's official Gatwick Web site, www.baa.co.uk/main/airports/gatwick. You can reach central London from Gatwick Airport by train, bus, or taxi.

By train

You have two choices of trains to take: the Gatwick Express and the Thameslink trains. The fastest and most convenient way to get into the center of the city is by taking the Gatwick Express train, which will take you directly from the airport into London's Victoria Station, located in the heart of London near Buckingham Palace. The Gatwick Express departs from the airport's South Terminal. Once you pass through customs, look for the signs directing you to the Gatwick Airport train station, which is inside the South Terminal. When you reach the ticketing area, you will find overhead monitors displaying the departure and arrival times from the airport train station for both the Gatwick Express and the Thameslink trains. You will see the lines to the ticket windows to the right of the overhead monitors where you may buy your train tickets or get travel information. You can use your credit card to charge your tickets at the ticket window. You might want to use an ATM machine at the airport to get British currency from your checking account before you board the train. You can find an ATM to your right once you reach the train ticketing area. Better yet, you can skip the long lines at the ticket window and go directly to the train, where you can

Gatwick Airport train station.

buy your Gatwick Express tickets from the staff on board the train for no additional fee with British currency or by credit card. To buy a round trip ticket, be sure to ask for a "return ticket."

The Gatwick Express trains depart and arrive at the platforms directly below the ticketing area. Take the escalator downstairs to reach platforms 1 and 2. Monitors

The Gatwick Express.

on the platform indicate the departure times for the trains. The journey on the Gatwick Express to London's Victoria Station from Gatwick Airport takes only 30 minutes. Gatwick Express trains depart daily from the airport's South Terminal from 5:20 a.m. until 6:20 a.m. at 20 and 50 minutes past the hour. The Gatwick Express operates every 15 minutes beginning at 6:50 a.m. The last train departs the Gatwick Airport Station at 1:35 a.m.

You can choose to buy a First Class fare or the less expensive Express Class for the Gatwick Express. The Gatwick Express coaches are clean and modern and have a number of seats with tables, where you can break out your trusty map to get your bearings. The Gatwick Express staff will pass through the cars and will stamp your ticket, or they can sell tickets if you have decided to buy your tickets on board. For more information, visit its Web site, www.gatwickexpress.co.uk.

The Thameslink train also runs between the South Terminal at Gatwick Airport, with stops at the London Bridge, Blackfriars, City Thameslink, Farrington, and King's Cross Thameslink train stations in central London. There are four trains departing Gatwick Airport each hour during the day. The fare is slightly less than the Gatwick Express, but the trip takes longer as the train makes more stops along the way. The Thameslink train is also a commuter service, and the cars are not as comfortable or modern as those on the Gatwick Express line. Check your map of London to see if your hotel is close to the London Bridge, Blackfriars, City Thameslink, Farrington, or King's Cross train stations. If so, you might want to take the Thameslink train into London instead of the Gatwick Express, which takes you to Victoria train station. Unlike the Gatwick Express, you must buy a ticket before you board the Thameslink train, either at the ticket window in the train station, or at one of the Thameslink ticket desks in the North and South Terminals. For more information, visit its Web site, www.thameslink.co.uk.

By bus

You can also take a bus into central London. Speedlink Flightline 777 offers non-stop service from Gatwick Airport to Victoria train station. The buses depart on the hour and the journey takes about an hour and a half, depending on traffic. At Victoria Train Station, you can then take a taxi or catch the Underground to your hotel. For more personalized service, Hotelink offers direct door-to-door mini-bus shuttle service between both Heathrow and Gatwick Airports and central London hotels. You can find Hotelink information desks in each terminal. If you make a reservation in advance, you can arrange for a Hotelink representative to meet your party. This is a particularly good transportation option for travelers needing assistance with wheelchairs or those with special needs. For more information, or to make reservations, check out its Web site, www.hotelink.co.uk.

By taxi

It is impractical and expensive to take a taxi from Gatwick Airport into central London. Unless there is a rail and bus strike, taxis are not a very good option. The trip can take well over an hour due to the heavy south London traffic. If you must take a taxi, there are signs in each terminal directing you to the taxi stand, called a "queue" in Britain. If you are planning on taking a taxi, it is best to make sure you have some British currency to the pay the taxi driver before you leave the Gatwick Airport station, although some taxis do take credit cards. You should ask the driver before you depart to see if he accepts credit cards.

Heathrow Airport

Heathrow Airport is one of the world's busiest international airports. About 64 million people flying on over 90 airlines pass through the airport each year. Heathrow Airport has four separate terminals, which are linked by underground passageways and people-mover sidewalks. Plans are under way for the construction of a fifth terminal. Heathrow is located about 15 miles west of London. Most United States airlines (with the noted exception of Delta Airlines) fly into Heathrow Airport. Heathrow Airport offers several easy transportation options to get you to the center of London by the Underground, railway, or bus. For more information on the airport and its services visit the airport's official Web site, www.baa.co.uk/main/airports/ heathrow.

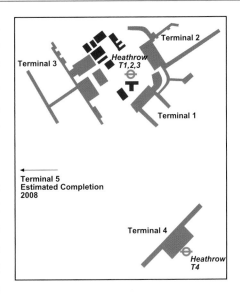

By train

By far the quickest way to get from Heathrow Airport to central London is by the Heathrow Express train. The Heathrow Express trains are sleek and modern and offer direct service from Heathrow Airport into London's Paddington train station, which is located north of Hyde Park. There is a Heathrow Express train station in the airport below terminal 4. Signs will direct you to the escalators, which will take you down to the railway platform. Note that this is a different station from the Heathrow Underground station. Directions to both are well marked. The Heathrow Express train then proceeds to the train station that serves Terminals 1, 2, and 3. The rail service is offered every fifteen minutes from 5:07 a.m. until midnight departing at 10, 25, 40, and 55 minutes past each hour. The entire trip from Heathrow Airport to London's Paddington Station takes only fifteen minutes. The Heathrow Express trains arrive and depart from platform 6 or 7 at London's Paddington train station. For more information, visit its Web site, www.heathrowexpress.co.uk. To get local currency, you can find an ATM machine in Terminal 2.

By Underground

The cheapest way to get from Heathrow Airport to central London is on the Tube. Heathrow Airport has two Tube stations, which serve the Piccadilly Line. The Underground can take you directly into the heart of London with convenient central stops, including Green Park, Piccadilly Circus, Leicester Square, Covent Garden, Holburn, Russell Square, and the King's Cross train station. Signs in the Heathrow Airport terminals will direct you to the escalators that lead down to the platforms, where you can catch the Tube into town. There is one Tube station serving Terminals 1, 2, and 3, which are connected with underground passageways and moving sidewalks.

Terminal 4, however, is on the south side of Heathrow some distance from the other terminals and has its own Tube station. The train then proceeds from Terminal 4 over to the station serving Terminals 1, 2, and 3 before heading off to central London. The Underground trains leave approximately every ten minutes from Monday through Saturday, 5:08 a.m. until 11:33 p.m., Sunday 5:58 a.m. until 10:46 p.m. The train makes a number of stops along the Piccadilly Line, and so the trip into the center of London takes approximately 50 to 60 minutes.

By bus

There are several companies offering bus service from Heathrow Airport into central London. There is a Central Bus Station serving Terminals 1, 2, and 3. There are signs indicating the way to the Central Bus Station terminals. A limited number of services additionally stop at Terminal 4. Hotelink offers direct door-to-door shuttle service between Heathrow Airport and Gatwick Airport and central London hotels. There are Hotelink information desks in each terminal. For more information, visit its Web site, www.hotelink.co.uk.

Airbus offers two bus lines departing from all four terminals that will carry you into London. One line goes to King's Cross Station, with stops at Bayswater, Marble Arch, Euston, and Russell Square. The other bus line goes to Victoria train station, with stops at Cromwell Road, Knightsbridge, and Hyde Park Corner. The stops on both lines are near Tube stations. The Airbus service is offered from 7:30 a.m. until 11:30 p.m., every 20 minutes at peak times, every 30 minutes off-peak, and hourly during the night. The trip by bus takes approximately 70 minutes, depending on traffic. In addition to these two lines, Airbus Direct offers delivery and pickup to and from various central London hotels and Heathrow Airport. Tickets can be purchased from the Airbus desks in Terminals 1, 3, and 4 or from the driver on the bus. For more information, visit its Web site, www.nationalexpress.com.

By taxi

The most expensive travel option is by taxi. There is taxi service from each of Heathrow's four Terminals. Look for the signs in each terminal directing you to the Taxi stand, called a "queue." The trip time takes from 45 minutes to an hour, depending on the traffic.

RECOMMENDED READING

Ashley, Mike *A Brief History of British Kings and Queens* Carroll & Graf (December 23, 2002)

Bamber, Judith, and H. Smith *Rough Guide to Walks in and Around London* Rough Guides (September 2003)

Best, Nicholas *London: In the Footsteps of the Famous* Bradt Travel Guides (June 2002)

Dorling, Roger W. *Eyewitness Top 10 Travel Guide to London* Kindersley Pub. 1st Ed. (February 1, 2002)

Duncan, Andrew *Walking London: Thirty Original Walks In and Around London* McGraw-Hill 2nd Ed. (January 11, 1999); *Secret London: Exploring the Hidden City, with Original Walks and Unusual Places to Visit* Interlink Publishing Group (September 2003)

Humleker, Ruth *London for the Independent Traveler* Marlor Press Inc. (March 1999)

Jones, Richard, and G. McDonald *Frommer's Walking Tours: London* Hungry Minds, Inc. 2nd Ed. (August 1995)

Kahn, Robert (Editor) *City Secrets: London* Little Bookroom (September 9, 2001)

Kettler, Sarah Valente and Carole Trimble *The Amateur Historian's Guide to Medieval and Tudor London* Capital Books Inc. (February 1, 2001)

Fodor *Fodor's London 2003* Fodors Travel Pubns. (August 27, 2002)

Frasier, Antonia (Editor of the series *A Royal History of England* with University of California Press November 6, 2000) Frasier, Antonia et al. *The Lives of the Kings and Queens of England*; John Clarke and Jasper Ridley *The Houses of Hanover and Saxe-Coburg-Gotha*; Andrew Roberts *The House of Windsor*; Maurice Ashley *The Stuarts*; Neville Williams *The Tudors*; Anthony Cheetham *The Wars of the Roses*; John Gillingham and Peter Earle *The Middle Ages*

Hibbert, Christopher *Queen Victoria: A Personal History* Basic Books; 1st Ed. (December 26, 2000); *The Story of England* Phaidon Press Inc. Reprint Ed. (March 1993); *Redcoats and Rebels: The American Revolution Through British Eyes* W.W. Norton & Company (April 2002); *The Virgin Queen: Elizabeth I, Genius of the Golden Age* Wesley Publishing Company (May 1992); *George III: A Personal History* Basic Books 1st Ed. (February 2000); *Queen Victoria in Her Letters and Journals* Sutton Publishing (May 2000); *Nelson: A Personal History* Perseus Publishing (June 1996); *The Lives of the Kings and Queens of England* University of California Press Revised Ed. (February 2000)

King, Greg *The Duchess of Windsor: The Uncommon Life of Wallis Simpson* Carol Pub Grp. (September 2000)

Lacey, Robert *Monarch: The Life and Reign of Elizabeth II* Free Press (May 2002); *Majesty: Elizabeth II and the House of Windsor* Avon Reprint Ed. (July 1983)

Leapman, Michael *London (Eyewitness Travel Guides)* DK Publishing Rev. Ed. (October 1, 1999)

Porter, Darwin and Danforth Prince *Frommer's London 2003* Frommer (September 13, 2002)

Shawcross, William *Queen and Country: The Fifty-Year Reign of Elizabeth II* Simon & Schuster (May 2002)

Steinbicker, Earl *Daytrips London* (Daytrips London, 7th Ed.) Hastings House Pub. (September 2003)

Steves, Rick, and Gene Openshaw *Rick Steves' London 2003* Avalon Travel Publishing (November 2002)

Strober, Deborah H., and G. S. Strober *The Monarchy: An Oral Biography of Elizabeth II* Broadway Books (January 2, 2002)

Weir, Alison *The Life of Elizabeth I* Ballantine Books (October 6, 1999); *The Six Wives of Henry VIII* Grove Press (April 2000); *Henry VIII: The King and His Court* Ballantine Books (October 29, 2002); *The Wars of the Roses*, Phebe Kirkham (ed.) Ballantine Books (July 1996); *Eleanor of Aquitaine: A Life* Ballantine Books (April 3, 2001); *The Princes in the Tower*, Fawcett Books Reprint Ed. (August 1995)

Wessex, HRH Edward *Edward Wessex's Crown and Country: A Personal Guide to Royal London* (Accompanying the PBS documentary series of the same name, September 2001)

Windsor, HRH Edward *A King's Story - The Memoirs of the Duke of Windsor* Prion Books (November 1998)

White, Andrew (Editor) *Time Out Book of London Walks* Penguin Books Penguin USA (October 2001)

Woodley, Roger *Blue Guide London* 17th Ed. W.W. Norton & Co. (August 2002)

Ziegler, Philip *King Edward VIII: A Biography* Knopf (January 1991)

Interior Photo Credits
All interior photographs by Robert S. Wayne, except the following: © Corbis pp.9, 93, 97, 98, 101(top). Detail from the Bayeux tapestry © Erich Lessing / Art Resource, NY p.61; Henry VIII © National Trust / Art Resource, NY p.69; Oliver Cromwell © Bridgeman-Giraudon / Art Resource, NY p.78; George III © Bridgeman-Giraudon / Art Resource, NY p.87; George IV © Scala / Art Resource, NY p.89. Elizabeth I © Bridgeman Art Library/Getty p.73. © PA Photos pp.90, 95, 96, 100, 101, 102, 103, 104, 105, 108, 109, 114, 117, 119, 131. ImageDJ Corp. pp.10, 41, 56, 57, 123, 128, 129, 139, 153, 167, 174.

ACKNOWLEDGEMENTS

I am deeply grateful for the help and support of my friends Mark Bishop, Tedi and Joel Godard, Rebecca Landers, Mark Wasley, Renny Hart, Jan Bolgla, Richard and Jane Robb for their review of endless drafts of this book, and to Brian and Barbara Sherman for test-driving the tours. Without their helpful suggestions this book would not have been possible. My special thanks to Her Majesty's Consul General Michael C. Bates, OBE, Kirstine Rushing Press and Public Affairs Office British Consulate-General Atlanta, the staff of London's Hotel St. Margaret, the staff of IPG–Chicago Review Press, and Stephanie Hobbs of PBI, Ltd., and the good folks at L.E.G.O. I am indebted to Kate and Mike Bandos of KSB Promotions, and Joan B. Peterson of Travel Publishers Association for their help and support.

ABOUT THE AUTHOR

Royal London in Context is the second in a series of guides for the independent traveler, *Europe in Context*, conceived and written by Robert S. Wayne and published by Independent International Travel, LLC. *Venice In Context* was first published in 2003. Author Robert S. Wayne is a graduate of the University of Georgia with a degree in Vocal Music Performance. He went on to earn a law degree. He is the former Managing Editor of the Georgia Journal of International and Compar-ative Law. The author spent two summers studying opera at the American Institute for Musical Studies in Graz, Austria. He is now an attorney living in Atlanta, Georgia, where he balances the demands of a busy law practice with extensive travel and writing. The project *Europe in Context* reflects his life-long passion for music, history, and art and his experiences in over twenty years of traveling independently and exploring the treasures of Europe. He is currently researching the forthcoming *Florence In Context the Independent Traveler's Guide to Florence.*

ABOUT THE NARRATOR

The *Europe In Context* series, including *Royal London In Context* is narrated by Joel Godard, a veteran New York actor, spokesman, and Voice/Over talent. He has worked in TV, film, and radio for many years and has done on-camera and Voice/Over work in numerous commercials. He worked as an NBC network staff announcer before becoming the announcer for *Dateline NBC* with Jane Pauley and Stone Phillips. He has been heard as the network announcer for recent NBC broadcasts of Macy's *Thanksgiving Day Parade* and the lighting of the great Christmas tree at Rockefeller Center. Currently, he is the announcer for NBC's *Late Night with Conan O'Brien*, where he frequently makes on-camera appearances in the show's comedy sketches. He is married to actress Tedi Dreiser Godard.

RETAIL ORDERING ON-LINE

You can buy on-line with confidence directly from
our secure Web site: europeincontext.com.

ORDERING BY MAIL
INDEPENDENT
INTERNATIONAL TRAVEL, LLC
201 Swanton Way
Decatur, Georgia 30030-3271
SAN: 254-6558

All orders will be shipped immediately on receipt of payment.
Or you can buy from your favorite retailer:
Amazon or Barnes & Noble

WHOLESALE ORDERING INFORMATION:

Independent International Travel LLC's *Europe In Context* series
is distributed to the trade by
Independent Publishers Group
814 North Franklin St.
Chicago, IL 60610
Phone: (312) 337-0747
Orders Only: (800) 888-4741
Orders: orders@ipgbook.com
Customer Service: frontdesk@ipgbook.com
Available also from Ingram, Baker and Taylor, and other fine wholesalers

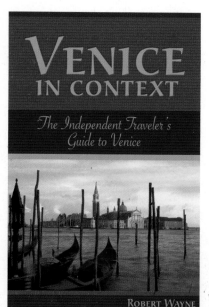

Praise for *Venice In Context* ISBN 0-9720228-7-2
the first book in the *Europe In Context* series:

Theodore K. Rabb, chairperson and professor of history, Princeton University "A very
useful guide for the first-time visitor to Venice."

Midwest Book Review "An evocative and
superbly conceptualized travel guide, not just
for the practical realities . . .but also for . . .
armchair travelers."

Durant Imboden, veniceforvisitors.com
"*Venice in Context* ...brings the guidebook and
audio tour together in a single, well-integrated
package."

Victor Cohen, RebeccaReads.com "*Venice In
Context* has paved the way toward a new generation of travel guides."

Library Journal "an exciting guide with a
unique approach sure to satisfy both new and
experienced visitors... A complete and satisfying
tour guide for travel planners or travel takers,
this is recommended for all travel collections in
both public and academic libraries."

192